CLASSIC SERMONS
ON WORLD
EVANGELISM

CLASSIC SERMONS

ON WORLD

EVANGELISM

Compiled by
Warren W. Wiersbe

Classic Sermons on World Evangelism
Hendrickson Publishers, Inc. edition
ISBN 1-59856-073-5

This edition is published by special arrangement with
and permission of Kregel Publications. Copyright ©
1999 by Kregel Publications, a division of Kregel, Inc.
P.O. Box 2607, Grand Rapids, MI 49501.

Printed in the United States of America

CONTENTS

List of Scripture Texts 6

Preface 7

1. Captured by a Vision 9
   Howard Frederick Sugden

2. A Quest for Souls 21
   George W. Truett

3. The First Preaching at Antioch 41
   Alexander Maclaren

4. Witnesses 51
   George Campbell Morgan

5. The Worldwide Gospel 65
   George H. Morrison

6. The Constraining Love of Christ 77
   John Henry Jowett

7. The Missionary Call of the Old Testament . 89
   John Daniel Jones

8. Review of the Whole Charge 101
   Joseph Parker

9. The Missionary's Charge and Charta 111
   Charles Haddon Spurgeon

10. The Missionary Debt 131
    Adoniram Judson Gordon

11. The Man of Macedonia 141
    Phillips Brooks

LIST OF SCRIPTURE TEXTS

Isaiah 6, Sugden 9

Jonah 1:1–3, Jones... 89

Jonah 3:2–5, Jones... 89

Matthew 10, Parker.. 101

Matthew 28:18–19, Spurgeon 111

Mark 16:15, Morrison 65

John 1:42, Truett 21

Acts 5:32, Morgan 51

Acts 7, 10, 16, Sugden 9

Acts 11:20–21, Maclaren 41

Acts 16:9, Brooks 141

Romans 1:14, Gordon 131

2 Corinthians 5:14, Jowett 77

PREFACE

THE *KREGEL CLASSIC SERMONS SERIES* is an attempt to assemble and publish meaningful sermons from master preachers about significant themes.

These are *sermons,* not essays or chapters taken from books about themes. Not all of these sermons could be called great, but all of them are *meaningful.* They apply the truths of the Bible to the needs of the human heart, which is something that all effective preaching must do.

While some are better known than others, all of the preachers whose sermons I have selected had important ministries and were highly respected in their day. The fact that a sermon is included in this volume does not mean that either the compiler or the publisher agrees with or endorses everything that the man did, preached, or wrote. The sermon is here because it has a valued contribution to make.

These are sermons about *significant* themes. The pulpit is no place to play with trivia. The preacher has thirty minutes in which to help mend broken hearts, change defeated lives, and save lost souls; he can never accomplish this demanding ministry by distributing homiletical tidbits. In these difficult days we do not need clever pulpiteers who discuss the times; we need dedicated ambassadors who will preach the eternities.

The reading of these sermons can enrich your spiritual life. The studying of them can enrich your skills as an interpreter and expounder of God's truth. However God uses these sermons in your life and ministry, my prayer is that His church around the world will be encouraged and strengthened by them.

WARREN W. WIERSBE

Captured by a Vision

Howard Frederick Sugden (1907–1993) was a gifted expositor and loving pastor with a winsome sense of humor and the ability to make the Scriptures come alive to the contemporary mind. During more than sixty years of service, he preached in conferences and churches in many parts of the world. He pastored three churches in Michigan, finishing his course as pastor of South Baptist Church, Lansing, where he served for thirty-five years. He also pastored Central Baptist Church, London, Ontario, Canada, for three years. A lover of good books, he built a large library and unselfishly shared his knowledge and wisdom with all who called upon him. He was "a pastor's pastor."

This message was delivered at the Moody Bible Institute Founder's Week conference in Chicago, on February 3, 1966.

Howard Frederick Sugden

1

CAPTURED BY A VISION

Isaiah 6; Acts 7, 10, 16

A FEW MOMENTS AGO, a giant 707 screamed out of the sky and came in on the runway out at O'Hare Field. It pulled up by that long piece of balcony and men and women moved out into the port. Its arrival and its flight were made possible because on a December day in 1903 two men with a strange glint in their eyes looked at an odd box that they had made. Inside that box was a twelve-horsepower engine. In a few minutes it would be wound up and started, and it would fly for fifty-nine seconds at the incredible speed of thirty miles per hour. It was a great day at Kitty Hawk. The clouds hung low over the infant airport, but these two men with a strange glint in their eyes had a vision. They never lived to see O'Hare Field, but they had a vision.

In the year 1759 a baby boy was born. Many baby boys were born that year, but not many you know about. This one you do know about. Nine years after he was born, his father died and he was left alone. But at twenty-two he was elected to the House of Commons. The name of William Wilberforce is well known today. He had a vision. He was captured by what God might do with him.

Now, this is a day of clouds, all kinds of clouds, and they hang low over the world tonight. There are clouds that threaten to destroy us. We are greatly concerned about world events. And when we turn from world events to the events in theology, we find another area of cloudiness and haze. Men tell us God is dead. They tell us that we can no longer trust in the living God, the God who created heaven and earth, and all that is in them. When we move out of the realm of theology, then we enter into the realm of the Word of God, and we find that this Word

9

must be handled with clever fingers to unwrap the husk of mythology to get at truth. These are days of clouds. I have only one concern, that God might this evening in some way move upon our hearts that we might be men and women captured by God and sent back to our homes different from when we came.

Abraham was captured by a vision. He did not have radio. He had no radar and no Gulf gas station to guide him. He just started out with a vision.

Moses endured. He endured sufferings and afflictions as the leader of his people. He endured because he was captured by a vision.

You remember dear old Caleb. He stood at the foot of a mountain Moses had promised him, though some long-necked giant looked out at him, Caleb, an old man now, cried out to Joshua, "I had a vision of this mountain. Now, therefore, I pray thee, give me this mountain" (see Josh. 14).

I don't know what your mountain may be, and I don't know anything about the giants that peek out through the crevices at you. But I do know this, that if you are captured with a vision, you will go home different from when you came and prayer will be answered in your soul.

Now, there are movements of God, and I would like to talk with you about four activities of God in giving men a vision. Someone said to Tennyson one day, "I have one desire in my life, that I will leave the world a better place than I found it." Noble, noble thought. Tennyson said, "That is strange. I have one desire in my life, and that desire is to see God." That is vision.

A Vision of Sovereignty

Isaiah 6 is a familiar chapter. I will not read it to you but only suggest that this was one of the most unusual periods in Israel's history. It was almost like today. They had some society! Do you know that the king that was on the throne had the first guided missiles? Why, his public works project had reached out over Palestine, and every newspaper carried the headlines about Uzziah, what a great man he was. There was a sense of security and a sense of well-being all up and down the land, and it rested in this king. Nothing could ever happen to a nation that had a king like this. And then it did! He died, and Isaiah was involved in it. He was one who knew all about Uzziah. They were friends. He knew about his public works project. No doubt he had been invited into the capitol to discuss with him Route 96, who knows? Isaiah's hopes that day were crushed.

With that simple background, let us read verse 1: "In the year that king Uzziah died I saw also the Lord sitting. . . ." No panic in heaven. God did not say, "Oh, what are we going to do now? This ruler on earth has died." You just can't imagine God pushing the panic button and saying "Help!" No, but they were pushing panic buttons on earth, and the whole nation was in distress and mourning. Isaiah went down to the temple. As he stood in the great rotunda and looked across and saw the bronze casket, and the hopes of a nation resting there, suddenly God moved in upon that scene and gave Isaiah a vision—-one that we must have if we are going to live in this day. He saw God seated. He was not in panic. He was not frantic. He was not nervous. He was seated.

The other day I came across a book by an old-fashioned Methodist who wrote it a hundred years ago. The first two messages in it were on the theme of Isaiah's vision, and he makes a little comment about this: "Think of it! Isaiah looked up and he saw a sovereign God seated upon the throne, and the skirts of His raiment covered the world. God was a sovereign God. Kings died and kings lived, and presidents move and presidents are elected by the hand of a sovereign God."

We get all worried, all disturbed up our way. The phone rings and someone says, "Mr. Sugden, what do you think about the war? Don't you think you should march somewhere?" I am marching. But I am marching hand in hand with the sovereign God who is not disturbed about earth's events, only as they are the fulfillment of His plans and His purposes.

I was reading Morrison's great new volume, *The Oxford History of the American People.* In the very opening chapters he makes this statement about the Virginia Colony: "The colony of Virginia lived because they believed God would not let them fall." It is good to know this today with Vietnam and Cuba and Castro. Khrushchev is sick now, so we don't need to be disturbed about him. God is on the throne! No wonder Julia Ward Howe, after going to Washington and watching our armies march, went home and wrote:

> Mine eyes have seen the glory of the coming
>   of the Lord;
> He is trampling out the vintage where the
>   grapes of wrath are stored;
> He hath loosed the fateful lightning of His
>   terrible swift sword;
> His truth is marching on.

I say, Hallelujah! The Christian marches with Him in His sovereignty. We need a vision of His sovereignty today.

A Vision of Glory

But this is not all. There is another vision. In Acts 7 there is a young man preaching a great sermon. Talk about the exposition of the Word of God, all you have to do is read Acts 7. I have always thought that good preachers would be popular, but this puts the lie to that. This one was not. As you read you find this man reaching back and gathering up Abraham and Moses and David, and the pageantry of the Old Testament unfolds. Isn't it good to read how the men in the early days handled the Word of God. The Lord Jesus talked about all that was written in Moses and the prophets and the writings concerning Him. He did not say we have to have a new approach. He just believed the record. And Stephen believed it.

As Stephen came to the conclusion of his message, he became very personal. He said, "You know, as I have traced our history you must recognize that throughout the years of God's dealing with us as a people, there has always been a resistance to truth. Our fathers killed Isaiah and they put Jeremiah in the pit. As they have done, so you will do." Some old fellow in the front nudged the one next to him and said, "How long are we going to put up with this preacher? This is too personal." The other fellow said, "Wait until he gets to the next stopping point and we'll pick up some sticks and stones." And that's what they did. When he made his next pause, they reached down for stones. The Word of God says in verses 54 and 55: "When they heard these things, they were cut to the heart, and they gnashed on him with their teeth. But he, being full of the Holy Ghost, looked up steadfastly into heaven, and saw the glory of God, and Jesus standing."

I have talked with all my Greek friends and they are not much help here, but one of them came close, I think. He said, "It could be that when Stephen saw the glory of God, the glory of God was Jesus." He looked up, he saw the glory of God, and he saw Jesus standing.

The last time the disciples saw Him, He was ascending. That is where Acts 1 closes as far as the Lord Jesus' visible presence is concerned. It is right there that the epistle to the Hebrews takes over, and four times in that epistle we read of the Lord Jesus being seated. He sat down in His relationship to redemption and to sin because He had settled forever the question of sin by His sufficient sacrifice upon the cross. The Lord Jesus is not dying today. Once He died, and "under an eastern sky, 'mid a rabble's cry, a Man went forth to die" for me. In relation to sin and redemption, the Lord Jesus is seated. But in relation to my need, He stands, because you see Him now in His priestly ministry.

I am quite sure He stood to encourage Stephen. I have always believed that as He looked down and saw this young man about to give his life as a martyr, He was standing there in the glory and saying to Stephen, "Go on!" And He strengthened him to go on, gave him the courage that normally he would not have had.

When I was a young man, we used to have some great teachers. I remember one day in class hearing Dr. Harold Paul Sloan tell about an experience he had in going to a conference of which he was a part. He had stood valiantly for the truth. I could just see him, with his shoulders lifted, his great head with white hair thrown back, standing for

God. But nobody appreciated it. Strange! When the day was over, he went down to the station to take the train, his little briefcase under his arm. Snow was blowing around the station, and as he stood waiting for the train to take him back home, he related to us, "I wanted to die. Then suddenly it seemed that I had a vision. I saw Wesley. He was drawing near to the Savior, and as he did, he said, 'Sloan's fed up. Sloan's quitting. He wants to die. Lord, if You will bring him home and give me his body, I'll go back and I'll fight the battles. With Your courage, we'll win the victory.'" Sloan continued, "Then I was back at the station, and I was ready to go on, encouraged, because the Lord was involved in my need."

Oh, how we need to see that here is One who is involved. He stood to encourage Stephen.

I have always believed that along with His standing to encourage Stephen, He was also standing to strengthen him, to give him the unusual strength that he needed in that hour. You see, this is the function of a priest. The Lord Jesus has two offices, you know. He is at the right hand of the Father an Advocate, for "if any man sin, we have an advocate with the Father" (1 John 2:1). Think of it! It does not say if any man cries, if any man weeps; it says if any man sins he has an Advocate. That is Christ's office, and that is for failure. He is a Priest for frailty. If in our frailty He comes to us, and in our need of strength He comes to us. It makes us to go through life not somehow, but triumphantly.

The first time I ever met Bishop Culbertson was at a conference. The day I arrived I went up to my little room with a fearful heart. I dropped my suitcase and looked around. There on the wall was the word that God had for me. It showed a picture of a man bowed down, and underneath it said, "Not somehow, but triumphantly." This is what He wants to do for us, and it works down where we live every day.

Several years ago, up in the thumb of Michigan, a mother had taken her two boys to their grandfather's house to hunt deer. It was evening when the two boys went out in the cornfield. They parted, and as they watched for a moving deer, suddenly one of them saw a movement. He raised his gun and blasted. Then he heard a cry and he knew instantly he had not shot a deer. He ran over and found his brother, dying. An ambulance was called, and perhaps no other scene could so wonderfully describe how God gives strength. The mother, who had been widowed some ten years before, sat in the ambulance that was scurrying down the roadway to the nearest hospital, with her young high school boy. He said, "Mom, I think it is the end for me. I don't think I'll survive. It must be that this is the way God wants it. Mom, will you sing for me?" She did. They had been up at Keswick the summer before and had learned our great Keswick hymn. As she finished singing he said, "Mother, will you sing that great rock song?" And there in the ambulance that mother sang to her dying boy:

> Thou art my Rock, O blessed Redeemer,
> Thou art my Refuge where I may hide;
> Thou art my Rock to shelter and bless me;
> Ever in Thee I safely abide.

You see, it is down where we live we need this strength. We need the vision that Stephen had when he saw the Lord God, the God of glory, giving strength to His own.

A Vision of Grace

But that is not all. There are four of these movements and they involve every area of the human life. In Acts 10 there is another vision. This is not a vision of sovereignty, such as Isaiah had. It is not a vision of strength or glory, such as Stephen experienced. This is a vision of grace.

All of you are aware that the opening chapters of Acts deal with the Lord Jesus and His movement in the church, and the Holy Spirit's work in the church among Jewish people. It began at Jerusalem and Judea. It had gone to Samaria, and now the church was standing in a position that was dangerous. It was in danger of becoming a Jewish sect. And right at this time, Cornelius, a Gentile, had a vision.

He was a good man. He would have been on the board in most churches. But he was not saved. He was a Gentile who had lived up to the light he had, and when a man lives up to the light he has, God gives him more light. This is the genius in missions. A vision came to Cornelius and said, "Send for Peter." How was he going to get to Peter? Peter was down at Joppa, thirty miles away.

At the very time that messengers were on the way, Peter was up on a housetop. His hostess was slow in getting the meal. He could smell the beef burgers cooking, and as he thought of food, he had a vision. It is amazing how the emphasis is upon hunger. Peter was hungry. But I am quite sure that when Luke wrote this, he saw in Peter's hunger more than the hunger that could be satisfied at the table in the dining room. He must have remembered that day when the Lord Jesus with His disciples went through Samaria. The disciples went into McDonalds to get hamburgers, and when they came back, they were shocked to see that the Lord Jesus was sitting on the well talking with a woman of Samaria. One of them broke open the sack and said, "Have one." And you know what He said. Peter never forgot it. The Lord said, "I have meat to eat that you men know nothing about. This lost woman has satisfied the hunger of my soul." Peter was hungry, but his hunger was for more than bread and meat.

While he thought and prayed, a sheet came down from heaven. I am glad it says a great sheet. I am afraid of skinny sheets. Through the years the church has been holding out skinny sheets for people. When God dropped a sheet, He dropped a great sheet. In it were clean and unclean animals and creeping things.

Dear old Dr. Ironside used to tell about his father when he was dying. He would say to his wife, "Tell me that story again." When she came to "creeping things," he would stop her and say, "That's where I got in. That's where I got in." That is the grace of God.

While Peter thought on these things, there was a rap, and the lady of the house went to the door. Three men stood there and said, "Is there a gentleman here by the name of Peter?" They were invited in, and they ate. The next day ten men traveled down the expressway, six Jewish men, Peter, and three Gentiles. When they arrived at Cornelius' house, there they were, Mr. and Mrs. Cornelius, and all the little Corneliuses. Cornelius said, "We are all gathered here to hear the word."

Do you know what Peter started out to say? He said, "I would like to give you a few simple statements about existentialism. That has helped so many people." No, he did not. He said, "I perceive that God is no respecter of persons, (Acts 10:34), and he told them about a Christ who had died, a Christ who had risen. He never had a chance to say, "Finally, brethren." Oh, Peter said, "This is a vision of what God is doing. He is breaking down walls, He is reaching to the uttermost part of the earth. He is taking in all men and women." We need this today. We have so many skimpy sheets, and we have made the gospel of Jesus Christ something over which we dispute, rather than that which we proclaim. Peter simply said to them, "Whosoever believeth in him shall receive remission of sins" (v. 43). He didn't even have a chance to give the invitation. Cornelius and his whole family stood up. "Oh," they said, "this is what we have been waiting for. Thank God, the gospel of the grace of God has reached to us."

A vision of grace. I need this. It is so easy for me to go in my office and sit down and think I am a scholar. I am not. It would be easy to just sit and delegate all the work and say, "Brethren, this is for you to do." But there are days when I take my little car and drive down the streets of my city, and as I drive I cry and say, "O God, that these people might know the grace that has been made available in Jesus Christ. We need a vision of grace. And I pray that I may have it."

A vision of sovereignty, a vision of glory, a vision of grace. But that is not all. If you have all this but do not have the last vision that God drops right down where we are on this great missionary day, we would miss it all.

A Vision of People

As you open Acts 16 you hear the roar of the sea and the swish of the waves. A man moves through the gloom, and as he reaches the edge of the sea he feels the spray in his face. Everything is pushed into this hour, every single thing in this chapter is pushed into it: friends he has consulted, circumstances, conditions, all pushed into this hour. Just as you have been pushed into this hour, just as you have been brought here tonight, Paul was brought to this hour. As he stands there in the night, a man stands over across the sea, and holding out his hand he cries, as only a man in need can cry. Have you ever heard a man in need cry? Oh, I pray you will hear a man in need cry, in your city, on your street, in your office, in your building. Oh, to hear the cry of a man in need and be moved by that cry. Why, there are people today who are getting emotionally upset over TV commercials, and they never bat an eye in the house of God! Just think of it.

This man cries, "Come on over, we need you." Paul cries back, "Get an IBM machine. Get a recorder. Get a gadget." No, he doesn't. Do you know what Paul has found? Paul has found in this a vision of a program that has been pushing its way into his heart, and God's program is always a person. This is God's program. He is not going to speak to anyone in your office unless He speaks through you. The woman next door is not going to hear about the Lord Jesus unless you realize that God's method is to use you as a living personality.

The church withers, dies, decays when people lose the wonder of the program of God. I wish it could be done with machinery. Wouldn't it be nice? But it can't be done that way. Do you know how I know it can't be done? Because there was a time when God gave to Israel the wonderful task of making His glory known as they marched for forty years. Then after they had gotten in the land and things were more settled, they brought up the ark. They said, "We have carried this thing around so long on our shoulders, let's get a '66 model. That should be pleasing to God." So they went out and got a '66 model, hydromatic, everything, and they loaded the ark of God. God reached down from heaven and said, "O man, don't you know. My glory, the wonder of Myself, can never be carried on by machinery. It has to be on human shoulders, the shoulders of men, the shoulders of women."

We need this vision. You cannot escape it tonight. You just cannot escape it. God does not have any other hands, He does not have any other feet but ours. God's program is a person. Surrender to, no, affirm, the will of God, and immediately move as Paul moved in his affirmation of God's will in his life.

All scripture is given by inspiration of God, and is profitable (2 Tim. 3:16).

A Quest for Souls

George W. Truett (1867–1944) was perhaps the best-known Southern Baptist preacher of his day. He pastored the First Baptist Church of Dallas, Texas, from 1897 until his death and saw it grow both in size and influence. Active in denominational ministry, Truett served as president of the Southern Baptist Convention and for five years was president of the Baptist World Alliance, but he was known primarily as a gifted preacher and evangelist. Nearly a dozen books of his sermons were published.

This sermon was taken from *A Quest for Souls,* published in 1917 by Harper and Brothers, a volume of sermons that Truett preached in an evangelistic crusade in Fort Wayne.

2

A QUEST FOR SOULS

And he brought him to Jesus (John 1:42).

THE BRINGING OF A SOUL to Jesus is the highest achievement possible to a human life. Someone asked Lyman Beecher, probably the greatest of all the Beechers, this question: "Mr. Beecher, you know a great many things. What do you count the greatest thing that a human being can be or do?" And without any hesitation the famous pulpiteer replied: "The greatest thing is, not that one shall be a scientist, important as that is; nor that one shall be a statesman, vastly important as that is; nor even that one shall be a theologian, immeasurably important as that is; but the greatest thing of all," he said, "is for one human being to bring another to Christ Jesus the Savior."

Surely, he spoke wisely and well. The supreme ambition for every church and for every individual Christian should be to bring somebody to Christ. The supreme method for bringing people to Christ is indicated here in the story of Andrew, who brought his brother Simon to Jesus. The supreme method for winning the world to Christ is the personal method, the bringing of people to Christ one by one. That is Christ's plan. When you turn to the Holy Scriptures, they are as clear as light, that God expects every friend He has to go out and see if he cannot win other friends to the same great side and service of Jesus.

"Ye shall be witnesses unto me," said Jesus, "both in Jerusalem, and in all Judea, and in Samaria, and unto the uttermost parts of the earth" (Acts 1:8). The early church went out and in one short generation shook the Roman empire to its very foundation. It was a pagan, selfish, sodden, rotten empire. Yet in one short generation, that early church had shaken that Roman empire from center to circumference and kindled a gospel light in every part of the vast domain. And they did it by the personal method. The men and the women and the children who loved Christ went out everywhere and talked for Christ in the hearing of those who knew Him not. The hearers became interested, followed on, and found out for themselves the saving truth that there is in Christ's gospel. Every Christian, no matter how humble, can win somebody else to Christ. You would not challenge that, would you? Let me say it again. Every Christian, however humble, can win somebody to Christ.

That is a most interesting and instructive story told of the nobly gifted Boston preacher, Dr. O. P. Gifford, who preached one morning to his congregation, making the insistence that it is the business, primary and fundamental, of Christ's people to go out constantly and win others to the knowledge of the Savior. And as he brought to bear his message upon his waiting auditors, with words that breathed and thoughts that burned, the minister came on to say: "Every Christian can win somebody to Christ." When the sermon was done and the people were sent away, there tarried behind one of his humblest auditors—probably the humblest, with reference to this world's goods, for she was a poor seamstress. She tarried behind to make her plea to the preacher that his sermon was overstressed.

Greatly moved she was, the preacher stated, as looking him in the face she said: "Pastor, this is the first time that I ever heard you when you seemed to be unfair." "Pray, wherein was I unfair?" he asked. Then she said: "You kept crowding the truth down upon us that every Christian could win somebody to Christ. Now, you did not make any exceptions, and surely I am an exception. Pray, tell me what could I do? I am but a poor seamstress, and I sew early and late to get enough to keep the wolf from the door for my fatherless children. I have no education and no opportunity, yet your statement was so sweeping that even I was included, and in that," she said, "I think you were unfair—the first time I ever knew you to be so." And then, when she had finished her vehement protest, he looked down at her in all her agitation, and said to her: "Does anybody ever come to your house?" She said: "Why, certainly, a few people come there." And then, waiting a moment, he said: "Does the milkman ever come?" "To be sure," she said. "Every morning he comes." "Does the bread man come?" "Every day he comes." "Does the meat man come?" "Every day he comes to my cottage." Then, waiting a moment for his questions to have their due effect, looking down earnestly at her, he said: "A word to the wise is sufficient," and he turned upon his heel, abruptly leaving her.

She went her way. The nightfall came and she went to her bed to ponder late and long the searching message she had heard that morning. Why, she had not even tried to win anybody to Christ. She had never made the effort. She claimed to be Christ's friend, yet had never opened her lips for Him at all. She will try, and she will begin with her first opportunity tomorrow, even with the coming of the milkman.

Accordingly she was up before the daylight came, there waiting, if haply she might speak to him some word concerning personal religion. When he greeted her, he made the remark that he had never seen her up quite so early before, and she stammered out some embarrassing reply, not saying what she came to say. Now he had left her, and the gate clicked behind him as he left. Then she summoned her strength and called him back. "Wait a minute," she pleaded, "I did have something to say to you." And when he tarried to hear it, she poured out her heart to him in the query: "Do you know Christ? Are you a Christian? Are you the friend and follower of that glorious Savior who came down from heaven and died that you might not forever die?" And fairly dropping his milk pails, he looked into her face with anguish in his own as he said to her: "Little woman, what on earth provoked you to talk to me like this? Here for two nights, madam, I have been unable to sleep. The burden of it all is that I am not a Christian, and I am in the darkness. If you know how to find the light, you are the one that I need, and you should tell me." And there, in a few brief minutes of conversation, she told him how she had found the light, and he walked in that simple path that she indicated for him.

Dr. Gifford goes on to tell us that before that year was out, that same little seamstress had won seven adults to Christ, not only to the open confession of Christ as their Savior, but to take their places promptly in His church. You can win somebody to Christ. Have you tried? Will you try? Won't you try, looking to God to guide and help you?

The text tells of a man who won somebody to Christ. The case of an ordinary man is this, and therefore he is chosen, for we are just ordinary people. This man Andrew is not Paul, the outstanding Christian of the centuries. He is not Apollos, that eloquent, winsome man who could compel people to listen to him, his words were so entrancing. He is just an ordinary, everyday, commonplace man. The Bible makes only three or four passing references to him. This man is the illustration we are to have tonight of the one person going out to win some other person to Christ. Let us fix our eyes upon him tonight and learn from the story something to help us.

Andrew here stands forth as one who has just found the Savior. How will he act? Two things stand out in response to that question: How will he act? First of all, Andrew is immediately interested that somebody else may be saved. Don't you like that? Isn't that a wonderful example for us? Immediately, this man Andrew is concerned that somebody else may be saved. Oh, there are different evidences, my friends, indicated in these Holy Scriptures, whereby we may pass upon this eternally consequential question, whether or not we have been born again. It may be that at one of these services we will group these scriptural evidences and focus them upon this question: "Have I been born again, and what are the scriptural evidences that I have been born again?" Certainly we might not be able to have a more interesting or profitable study. But whether we shall give ourselves or not to such service, here stands out for us one shining fact like a mountain peak: If one is born again, that one is concerned that somebody else may be saved.

"If any man have not the Spirit of Christ, he is none of his" (Rom. 8:9). And the spirit of Christ is the spirit of compassionate anxiety that lost people may be saved. Now, Andrew evinces his concern, straightway after he finds the Messiah, that somebody else may find that same blessed, forgiving Savior.

Years ago, I was preaching in a series of daily meetings like these, and one Sunday morning, when I made the call for those who would confess Christ to come forward and remain, there came a group down the aisles and a number waited to be received into the church. When I came to question them about their coming into the church, I came presently to a humble German girl, a servant in one of the families. She was not long from the old country, and her English was barely intelligible as we listened to it. I said to her: "My child, why do you wish to join the church?" In her broken English, she made her reply to my question, and her English was so bad that it was well-near impossible for us to understand just what she was saying. Then I said to her: "My child, if you won't mind, I will ask you to wait a week, and let us talk with you quietly and carefully, as is the custom with all the young people that come into the church. We would be careful about this great step. The church is for those who have found Christ as their Savior, who know the way, and too much care can hardly be exercised at that point. I will just ask, if you don't mind, that you will wait and let us talk it over that no mistake may be made." She readily assented to my proposal, and I passed to the next case.

When I was questioning him presently the child broke out in a sob audible to those in the rear of the large auditorium. All of us were immediately embarrassed. Evidently I had grieved her. I turned back to her frankly and said: "Why, my child, I did not mean to grieve you by asking that you wait. That is not anything unusual. The church is doing that sort of thing here constantly. We are asking that the young people talk with the pastor and with the parents carefully before they come into the church. Coming into the church is one of the greatest steps for a human soul, and it ought to be taken with much deliberation and wisdom. It was for your good, my child, and it is not anything unusual that you are asked to wait." She said, with better English now: "Oh, sir, it is not that that makes me cry! I forgot. I cried because my brother here in this city is such a wild boy. He is lost, and my heart is breaking. I am so concerned that he shall be saved. Won't you ask everybody here today to join me in one prayer that my poor, lost, sinful brother may be saved? That is what made me cry." And the dear old senior deacon spoke up and said: "Pastor, we had better take her into the church now. She knows the way, and we need not wait another week."

She did know the way. There was the outflashing in that conversation, in that last moment, of her deep knowledge of a forgiving Savior, and all that audience was swept with her tremulous appeal. They knew, every Christian there, that this woman knew the Lord because of her heart's longing for others to be saved.

There was another point about this man Andrew, strikingly suggested, when he found the Savior, and that point is that he went straight home to get his first work in for his Savior. Now, don't you like that? He went straightway to get in his first work for the great Savior whom he had just found in his own home. He went after a difficult case, let me tell you. He went after his own brother Simon. Rash and headstrong and impulsive was that man Simon. Yet plain Andrew, a weakling compared with Simon, went after that big, strong brother, nor did he cease until he had brought him to Christ.

Oh, if the limits of this hour allowed, I would like, my brothers, to pour out my heart in a plea for home religion. There is an old saying that comes to mind just here: "The shoemaker's wife is the worst shod person in the village." Oh, if I might pour out my heart for a moment in a plea that our homes be ordered like they ought to be in the realm of religion! If there be one place, let me say it to the parents, where you should put your best foot forward for Christ, it should be in your families. I tell you, that is an indictment against a father if his own boy does not believe in his religion. I tell you that is an indictment against a mother if her own girl does not believe: "My mother is the best Christian in all the world." Oh, that our religion in our homes shall be outshining and congruous and consistent, even after the highest and most heavenly fashion! The accent, in my humble judgment, that most of all needs to be pronounced this night, throughout this whole country, from border to border, is an accent on the religion of our homes. As goes the home, so shall go everything in the social order. The citadel, both for church and for state, is the home. If we shall have the right kind of homes, then shall everything in the social order be conserved and saved. But if our homes shall be beaten down and unraveled and frazzled out by every superficial and foolish thing—God save the mark!—the nation is doomed and the land shall be lost.

I wonder what your answer would be, as I look into the faces of Christian parents now, and ask you this simple question: Do you have family prayer at your house? Why don't you have it? You might have measured off to you one round thousand years in which to get up your reasons why a Christian parent should not have family prayer in his house, and when the thousand years had passed, you would come back without the semblance of even one reason. Oh, men and women who love Christ, with your children growing about you, or already fairly grown, is it possible that human life—invested as it is with such sacred meanings and opportunities and responsibilities—shall go passing away, and the most chief place of all to get in your witness for Christ, even under your own roof, shall be overlooked and lost! One of the most menacing signs that you can find in any community, if you are able to find it there, is the decay of family prayer in such community.

I am thinking now of two homes. To the first was I summoned one morning to the burial of their only child. She was a beautiful girl of some fifteen summers. They were not members of my congregation, but of another. However, their minister was absent, and therefore, I was summoned to conduct the funeral. I came to the splendid-looking home, and a vast concourse of people were in and about the house. I asked that I might see the family, and I was taken down the long hall and into the quiet room where the brokenhearted parents sat. As tactfully as I could, I began to find my way to an apprehension of the situation that I might the better speak in the funeral service to be had a few moments later. I found in response to questioning, presently, that both of these parents were professed Christians. Then I ventured to tell them that earth had no sorrow that heaven cannot heal, and that they must refuse to turn aside into the abyss of despair and brokenheartedness because they had a Savior, and they were His friends.

By this time the mother was on her feet and said: "Sir, I have something to tell you that has utterly broken our hearts." I waited to hear what it was, and then she said: "That beautiful girl yonder in her casket, our only child, has been here in our home these fifteen years. Yet, in all these years, though her mother is a Christian and her father is a Christian—in all these years that child never heard either one of us pray one time, sir." And then she waited a moment more and said: "Sir, our horrible fear is that it was not well with the child and that her blood will be on our garments." Will you say that it was not? Oh, cruelty of cruelties, inconsistency of inconsistencies, that a child should be in a Christian home fifteen years and never hear the voice of a parent one time lifted in prayer!

There was another home of which I would speak. I pleaded with the people one morning several years ago, begging them that they put first things first, and that the men who were Christians would pause at the breakfast table for a little season of prayer with the loved ones around them. Or, perhaps, in the evening time when the day was done, they would gather the circle about them, and speak with the great King and Savior in grateful acknowledgment and in continual plea for His mercies to be granted them. Numbers that morning said that they would change their ways. One outstanding businessman, whose voice was often heard in the city, searched me out and said: "Oh, I have lived miserably far from what is consistent and right. I will turn over a new leaf tonight. Family prayer shall be at my house tonight and every night henceforth."

I follow it just a moment more. The next morning, as I crossed the city, I saw his only son about fifteen or sixteen years of age, and as I was traveling rapidly along, the son summoned me. When he reached me, I saw in his face that there was a deep battle of some sort going on, and I said: "What is it, my boy, that I can do for you?" And then he looked down with face averted, and then looked up with his face covered with tears, and said: "You ought to have been at our house last night." "What happened at your house, my boy? I would like to know." He said: "Oh, you should have been there. Papa prayed last night! Papa had sister and me called into the room, and Papa sobbed as he told us he had not lived like a Christian father ought. Papa asked sister and me to forgive him. Neither of us could talk. We did not know what to say. Both of us cried. Papa asked mother to open the Bible for him, and he tried to read it, but he could not. Then papa knelt down and prayed, mostly about himself, and then he said when he got up: 'Children, Papa is going to live a different life from this time on.'"

Then the boy said: "I went to my room and could not sleep." I said: "Why couldn't you sleep, my boy?" And then, as he leaned over on my shoulder, he said: "I found out last night that I am a sinner and that I am lost. You do not know how I wanted to see you that you might tell me what to do." We turned into a little store house that was vacant, and there, in a few words, I told the lad how it is that Jesus saves a sinner. The lad made his simple, honest surrender and was saved that very Monday morning. You should have heard him the next Sunday morning when the pastor said: "Tell us, my boy, what started you in this upward way?" He looked across at his father on the other side of the house and said: "Papa's prayer last Sunday night started me in the upward way."

Oh, I know it is difficult to have family prayers, my men and women! I know it is difficult, but listen to this:

Everything on this earth worthwhile costs, and you and I must not, dare not, thrust back into some little inconsequential corner in our lives the thing most chief and commanding that God has appointed for the winning of the world to God.

There is another point for our consideration in the case of this man.Andrew. Andrew's act magnifies the place and the power of personal work in the winning of lost people to Christ—the place and power of personal work—and just there are several suggestions for our consideration. There can be no substitutes for personal work. Jesus is depending one on His friends to get His gospel made known to a gainsaying and unbelieving world. He is dependent on His friends. That is His own divinely appointed method. There can be no substitutes for personal work! Life must make its impact upon life.

Now, everybody seems to understand that, I have sometimes thought, better than the church of God understands it. The businessmen understand the power of personal work. They send out their drummers up and down the land to look into the faces of their customers, real or prospective, and explain their wares. And certainly the politicians understand the power of personal work. You let a great issue be on, city or state or national, with two virile parties each contending for supremacy, and you will observe that the champions of these parties send their spokesmen, their representatives, to look their fellowmen in the face and argue and plead and explain, if haply they may win their votes. Oh, will the church of God fail to lay to heart that the chief instrumentality, humanly speaking, for the winning of the world to Christ is the power of personal work?

There can be no substitute for personal work, none at all. Elisha may send his servant Gehazi with the prophet's own staff back yonder to the chamber where the dead boy lies, saying to his servant: "Put my staff on that boy and see if it won't bring him to life." The instructions may be carried out, but the boy will remain in the cold grip of death. Elisha, the prophet, himself must go and stretch his own body, warm and pulsing, on the cold body of that dead boy. Elisha himself must make the impact of life upon that dead body.

The Divine Master of life Himself gave an emphasis to personal work beyond anything that I can describe in my simple discourse this evening. Jesus preached His most chief sermon on the new birth to just one man. My fellowmen, if Jesus thought it worthwhile to have just one for His congregation, and there do His best work, surely the servant shall not be greater than his Master. And when Jesus came to preach His sermon on eternal life, He preached it yonder to a woman at the well of Samaria—a poor drab of a woman, about whose character the less said the better—yet she had a soul that was to live forever. When she came to that well to draw water therefrom, Jesus had His opportunity, and with words tactful and honest and faithful, He found His way to that woman's conscience, and at the right time revealed Himself as the forgiving Savior to her. Jesus gave His best service for one soul.

Listen to Him yonder as He tells the story of the shepherd leaving his ninety-nine sheep safely housed in the sheep cote. Ninety-nine of them were safe, but one was missing. He left the ninety-nine safely housed in the sheep cote and went out after that missing sheep, over the hills and mountains with his feet pierced by stones and thorns, searching, looking for that one missing sheep. Nor did he give up his quest until that sheep was found. The shepherd then brought it back and put it in the sheep cote with the others. What is Jesus saying in this pungent parable? "Oh, my church," the compassionate Savior says, "go out and seek earnestly until that lost sheep is found!" He is saying just that.

Now, all experience and all observation confirm the point that I am seeking to make, that there can be no substitutes for personal work. How shall we save our churches? My fellow Christians, there is one sure way, and that is that our churches be great lifesaving stations to point lost sinners to Christ. The supreme indictment that you can bring against a church, if you are able in truth to bring it, is that such church lacks in passion and compassion for human souls. A church is nothing better than an ethical club if its sympathies for lost souls do not overflow, and if it does not go out to seek to point lost souls to the knowledge of Jesus.

But now I come to a practical question. How may you and I win sinners to Christ as did Andrew of old? That is entirely practical. Let us focus our thoughts for a moment on the practical question: How may you and I, like Andrew, win people to Christ? There are several suggestions to be given in response to that question. First of all, let us magnify the Word of God and its Author, the Divine Spirit Himself. We are to magnify both the Word of God and the Author of such Word, namely the Holy Spirit Himself. The one is our sword, and the other is our power. We are to take this Word of God and deliver to the lost world about us the message of this Word of God concerning Jesus and the relation of humanity to Him.

Our message is made out for us, fortunately: "Preach unto it the preaching that I bid thee" (Jonah 3:2). "Preach the Word." The Word of God is to be proclaimed. The Word of God is to be avowed. The Word of God is to be declared. The Word of God is not bound. The Word of God will take care of itself, if only it be faithfully proclaimed. You and I are to come with this Word of God, and without mincing or reservation, are to tell men everywhere that outside of Jesus Christ they are lost and shall never meet God in peace if they are not forgiven by this Divine Savior. We are to declare that, and the Lord, in the power of His Spirit, shall apply and shall bring to pass such results as in His wisdom and mercy He deems best.

Nor is that all. As we give ourselves to the task of winning souls to Christ, we are with all diligence and devotedness to seek the guidance and power of the Divine Spirit Himself at every step. He will guide and help us. You do not have to see the man tomorrow by yourself—that difficult man. The talk you are to have with him is not to be in your own strength alone. Beside you shall stand the omnificent Savior, and going with you shall be the counsel and power of His Spirit. You do not have to see that woman in your own poor, unaided wisdom. You are to do the best you can, leaning on the Arm Everlasting, and God's wisdom and God's power clothed upon from His Spirit shall accompany your simple, honest effort.

Again, if you and I are to win people to Christ, then we are to use, like Andrew did, the power of personal testimony. When Andrew found his Savior, he said: "Brother, listen! I have found the Messiah. Let me tell you about Him." And then, with words that thrilled and burned, Andrew told his brother what he had tasted and seen and felt of Jesus, the long-looked-for Messiah. My fellow Christians, there is nothing else human quite so powerful as the power of an earnest personal testimony concerning Jesus' experience in your own life, as you tell somebody else what Jesus has been and consciously is to you yourself. You let some man in this audience come down this aisle and stand up and tell us: "This very day I have had definite dealings with God, and know it," and every ear is alert to catch what he says. There is no power like the power of personal testimony. You can tell that neighbor or friend how you heard Christ's voice and how you responded. You can tell that person what He said to you and what He did. You can share with that person what you have seen and experienced of His grace and love in your own little life. Tell that experience to somebody without delay.

But that is not all. There is no human power like the power of personal love as we go out to win people to Christ. Oh, do we care for the people around us who are lost? Do we really care? Of old there issued from the lips of one sorely pressed this plaintive cry: "No man cared for my soul." Are there men and women in Fort Worth who, if we could get at what they think, would say this to us: "They have their churches and their preachers and their Christians numbering many, but nobody ever cared for my soul?" Is there somebody in this community, lost and groping like a blind man for the wall, not ready to die, not ready to live, who in truth could say to us: "I have lived these long years, but nobody ever said that he cared for my soul?" Make that impossible as these days pass. Go with your word of witnessing and pleading and love, and go without delay. There is nothing so powerful in all this world as the power of love. Everybody ought to know the thirteenth chapter of 1 Corinthians by heart, and in its gracious spirit every one of us ought to live every day: "Though I speak with the tongues of men and of angels, and have not [love], I am become as sounding brass, or a tinkling cymbal" (v. 1).

Do we love lost sinners? Do we care for the young men about us who are coasting the downward road? Do we care for the people whose toil is rigorous and whose lot in life is hard? Do we care for businessmen and professional men who are sidestepping with reference to the supreme things, namely, the things of God and the soul and eternity? Do we love these people well enough to go to them and earnestly and alone say to them: "Is it well with your soul?" There is no power in human life like the power of love. The prayer that the psalmist of old prayed is the prayer that you and I ought to pray: "Enlarge my heart" (Ps. 119:32). He did not pray that his head might be enlarged. "Enlarge my heart," for out of the heart are the issues of life.

One of the most heart-moving conversions that I have ever known I witnessed years ago in my home city during the holiday period in midwinter. There reached me the message that a little Sunday school boy in one of our mission Sunday schools had been accidentally shot by his little neighbor friend. I hurried to the humble home as fast as I could go and found the unconscious little fellow in the hands of two skillful doctors as they sought to diagnose the case. After awhile, when they had finished their diagnosis and treatment, I asked them what of the case, and they said: "He will not live. The shot is to death." I asked them if he would recover consciousness, and they answered that he might. They also stated that he might live two or three days, or he might not live until morning.

I went back the next day, for this first day the boy's father was in the stupor of a terrible drunkenness. A greathearted and kindly father he was, too, when he was sober. Oh, the tragedy that many of these bighearted, capable men allow their lives thus to be cajoled and cheated and destroyed by some evil habit!

Anyway, I went back the next day, and the father was sobering up. He was a fine workman in a harness and saddlery establishment. He was sobering up, and the agony of his case was something pitiful to behold. He would walk the floor, and then he would pause, as the tears fell from his face, while he looked on that little suffering boy, nine or ten years of age.

I sat down beside the boy and waited for awhile. Presently the child opened his eyes, and the little fellow was conscious. His eyes were intelligent. His lips moved as he spoke my name, for he had frequently heard me speak in the mission where he went to Sunday school. I bent over him, and the father came and sobbed and laughed as he observed the consciousness that had come to his little boy. And the father stroked the little fellow's face and kissed him with all the affection of a mother, and said, as he laughed and cried: "My little man is better, and he will soon be well."

The little face was clouded as he feebly whispered, saying: "No, Papa, I will not get well." And then the father protested, as he said: "You will get well, and I will be a good man and will change my ways." The little fellow's face was clouded, and he kept trying to say something. I reached for the man to bend over to catch it, and this is what we did catch, after awhile: "When I am gone, Papa, I want you to remember that I loved you, even if you did get drunk."

That sentence broke the father's heart. He left the room, unable to tarry any longer. A few minutes later, I found him lying prone upon his face there upon the ground behind the little cottage sobbing with brokenness of heart. I got down by him and sought to comfort and help him. And he said: "Sir, after my child loves me like that, oughtn't I to straighten up and be the right kind of a man?" I said: "I have a story ten thousand times sweeter than that to tell you. God's only begotten Son loved you well enough to come down from heaven and die for you, Himself the just, for you the unjust, that He might bring you to God. Won't you yield your wasting, sinful life to Him, utterly and honestly, and let Him save you His own divine way?" And then and there he made the great surrender.

You should slip into one of our prayer meetings some night when the men and women talk about what Christ has done for them. One of the most appealing and powerful testimonies you would ever hear is the testimony of this harness workman as he stands up, always with tears on his face, to tell you that love brought him home when everything else had failed. They criticized him because he drank. They scolded him because he drank. They railed at him because he drank. They pelted him with harsh words because he drank. But a little boy said: "Papa, I love you even if you do get drunk." Love won the day when everything else had failed. Oh, my fellowmen, when everything else shall fail, "[love] never faileth" (v. 8). Do you love these lost men and women of Fort Worth? Then, I pray you, in the great Master's name, go and tell them that you care for them, and tell it before another sun shall sink to rest in the far west tomorrow evening.

Long enough have I talked, but I gather up as best I can all I should say for a final moment of appeal. Here it is: Oh, my fellow Christians, let us see to it that you and I, like Andrew, do our best to win people to Christ! What argument shall I marshal to get us to do that thing right now, and to get us to do that thing as we never did it before. What argument shall I marshal to get us to do that thing these passing days, linking our lives with God with a devotion, and giving ourselves with a humility and a personal appeal, such as we never knew before? What arguments shall I marshal to get us to do that right now? Shall I talk about duty? Then this is our first duty. And what a great word that word duty is! Robert E. Lee was right, that matchless man of the South, when he wrote to his son saying: "Son, the great word is duty." Shall I talk about duty? My fellow Christians, your duty and mine—primal, fundamental, preeminent, supreme, tremendously urgent—is that we shall tell these around us that we want them saved.

Shall I talk about happiness? Oh, was there ever another happiness on this earth comparable to this—the hearing from the lips of some soul the glad confession that you had said the word to win such soul to Christ? There is no happiness on this earth comparable to that.

Shall I talk about responsibility? What shall I say about responsibility? Your responsibility and mine for these souls about us lost is a responsibility big enough to stagger God's archangel. You are your brother's keeper. What if you neglect him, and he shall die in his sins? If you shall neglect him, and he shall die in his sins when you might have won him, then it shall turn out that you are your brother's spiritual murderer. Men can be killed by neglect. Women can be killed by neglect.

A while ago there was condemned to death in England a notorious criminal, one of the hardest in all the records of crime. Minister after minister sought to get into his cell before the man's execution to talk to such man about God and the hereafter, but he steadfastly refused see any minister. Presently, one somehow got into the cell, and began to talk with him, and the poor man, condemned to be executed tomorrow, realized that he was talking at last with a minister of the gospel. The minister brought to bear his mightiest appeal to that man to turn to God, even in those last waiting hours. The man was stolid and was utterly indifferent, and presently the minister said to the man: "Don't you realize that in a few hours more your life shall be taken, and you shall be in another world?" He said: "Quite well, sir, do I realize that my life will be taken, but whether there is another world or not, I do not know, and I have not any concern about that." And then the minister urged and remonstrated and pleaded, and at last the condemned man rose up and said to him: "Sir, if I believed like you say that a man dying without Christ is lost, and shall be lost forever—if I believed that and had your chance—I would crawl on my knees to tell the men of England, before it is too late, to repent of their sins and turn to God."

Oh, do we believe it, that these men and women about us, and the dear young people under our own roofs, and the devoted husbands, beside whom walk as gentle, Christian wives—do we believe that these men are lost and that these young people are lost? Do we believe it? Then, I pray you, even as I summon myself, let us go to them in the right spirit, pleading with God to teach us, to empower us, to enable us to plead that now, before the day is gone, they may repent of sin and be saved forever.

My message is done when I shall have asked one question. Mark it: Do the Christian men and women listening to me, down in their hearts, really wish that sinners shall be saved during these days of special meetings? Probably hundreds here present answer me back: "Sir, that is our deep wish, that sinners may be saved." But I am going to make it stronger than that. Do the Christian men and women listening to me say, "Sir, I promise you, yes, sir, I promise God, and in the presence of God and of angels and men, I declare my promise, not only do I desire to see sinners saved in these special meetings, but I will try myself, frail as I am and weak as I am—I will try myself, like Andrew, to win somebody to Christ?" Do you say: "That is my wish, sir, and that is my purpose, God helping me"? Everyone who says that stand to your feet, and go and do likewise.

NOTES

The First Preaching at Antioch

Alexander Maclaren (1826–1910) was one of Great
Britain's most famous preachers. While pastoring the
Union Chapel, Manchester (1858–1903), he became
known as "the prince of expository preachers." Rarely
active in denominational or civic affairs, Maclaren
invested his time in studying the Word in the original
languages and sharing its truths with others in sermons
that are still models of effective expository preaching. He
published a number of books of sermons and climaxed
his ministry by publishing his monumental *Expositions
of Holy Scripture*.

This message was taken from *The Secret of Power,*
published by Funk and Wagnalls Company in 1902.

Alexander Maclaren

3
THE FIRST PREACHING
AT ANTIOCH

And some of them were men of Cyprus and Cyrene, which, when they were come to Antioch, spake unto the Grecians, preaching the Lord Jesus. And the hand of the Lord was with them: and a great number believed, and turned unto the Lord (Acts 11:20–21).

THUS SIMPLY DOES the historian tell one of the greatest events in the history of the church. How great it was will appear if we observe that the weight of authority among critics and commentators sees here an extension of the message of salvation to Greeks (that is, to pure heathens), and not a mere preaching to Hellenists (that is, to Greek-speaking Jews born outside Palestine).

If that be correct, this was a great stride forward in the development of the church. It needed a vision to overcome the scruples of Peter, and impel him to the bold innovation of preaching to Cornelius and his household. As we know, his doing so gave grave offense to some of his brethren in Jerusalem. But in the case before us, some Cypriote and African Jews—men of no note in the church, whose very names have perished, with no official among them, with no vision nor command to impel them, with no precedent to encourage them, with nothing but the truth in their minds and the impulses of Christ's love in their hearts—solve the problem of the extension of Christ's message to the heathen. Quite unconscious of the greatness of their act, they do the thing about the propriety of which there had been such serious question in Jerusalem.

This boldness becomes even more remarkable if we notice that the incident of our text may have taken place before Peter's visit to Cornelius. The verse before our text, "They which were scattered abroad upon the persecution

41

that arose about Stephen traveled . . . preaching the word to none but unto the Jews only" (v. 19), is almost a verbatim repetition of words in an earlier chapter. It evidently suggests that the writer is returning to that point of time in order to take up another thread of his narrative contemporaneous with those already pursued. If so, three distinct lines of expansion appear to have started from the dispersion of the Jerusalem church in the persecution—namely, Philip's mission to Samaria, Peter's to Cornelius, and this work in Antioch. Whether prior in time or not, the preaching in the latter city was plainly quite independent of the other two. It is further noteworthy that this, the effort of a handful of unnamed men, was the true "leader"—the shoot that grew. Philip's work, and Peter's so far as we know, were side branches, which came to little. This led on to a church at Antioch, and so to Paul's missionary work and all that came of that.

The incident naturally suggests some thoughts bearing on the general subject of Christian work, which we now briefly present.

The Spontaneous Impulse

Persecution drove the members of the church apart. As a matter of course, wherever they went they took their faith with them and, as a matter of course, spoke about it. The coals were scattered from the hearth in Jerusalem by the armed heel of violence. That did not put the fire out, but only spread it, for wherever they were flung they kindled a blaze. These men had no special injunction "to preach the Lord Jesus." They do not seem to have adopted this line of action deliberately or of set purpose. They believed and, therefore, spoke. A spontaneous impulse, and nothing more, leads them on. They find themselves rejoicing in a great Savior-Friend. They see all around them men who need Him, and that is enough. They obey the promptings of the voice within and lay the foundations of the first Gentile church.

Such a spontaneous impulse is ever the natural result of our own *personal possession* of Christ. In regard to worldly good the instinct, except when overcome by higher motives, is to keep the treasure to oneself. But even in the natural sphere, there are possessions that to have are to long to impart, such as truth and knowledge. And in the spiritual sphere, it is emphatically the case that real possession is always accompanied by a longing to impart. The old prophet spoke a universal truth when he said: "His word was . . . as a fire shut up in my bones, and I was weary with forbearing, and I could not stay" (Jer. 20:9). If we have found Christ for ourselves, we shall undoubtedly wish to speak forth our knowledge of His love. Convictions that are deep demand expression. Emotion that is strong needs utterance. If our hearts have any fervor of love to Christ in them, it will be as natural to tell it forth as tears are to sorrow or smiles to happiness. True, there is a reticence in profound feeling, and sometimes the deepest love can only "love and be silent," and there is a just suspicion of loud or vehement protestations of Christian emotion, as of any emotion. But for all that, it remains true that a heart warmed with the love of Christ needs to express its love and will give it forth as certainly as light must radiate from its center or heat from a fire.

Then, true *kindliness of heart* creates the same impulse. We cannot truly possess the treasure for ourselves without pity for those who have it not. Surely there is no stranger contradiction than that Christian men and women can be content to keep Christ as if He were their special property, and have their spirits untouched into any likeness of His divine pity for the multitudes who were as sheep having no shepherd. What kind of Christians must they be who think of Christ as "a Savior for me," and take no care to set Him forth as "a Savior for you?" What should we think of men in a shipwreck who were content to get into the lifeboat, and let everybody else drown? What should we think of people in a famine feasting sumptuously on their private stores, while women were boiling their children for a meal and men fighting with dogs for garbage on the dunghills? "He that withholdeth corn, the people shall curse him" (Prov. 11:26). What of him who withholds the Bread of Life, and all the while claims to be a follower of the Christ, who gave His flesh for the good of the world?

Further, *loyalty to Christ* creates the same impulse. If we are true to our Lord, we shall feel that we cannot but speak up and out for Him, and that all the more where His name is unloved and unhonored. He has left His good fame very much in our hands, and the very same impulse that hurries words to our lips when we hear the name of an absent friend calumniated should make us speak for Him. He is a doubtfully loyal subject who, if he lives among rebels, is afraid to show his colors. He is already a coward and is on the way to be a traitor. Our Master has made us His witnesses. He has placed in our hands, as a sacred deposit, the honor of His name. He has entrusted to us, as His most select sign of confidence, the carrying out of the purposes for which on earth His blood was shed, on which in heaven His heart is set. How can we be loyal to Him if we are not forced by a mighty constraint to respond to His great tokens of trust in us, and if we know nothing of that spirit which said: "Necessity is laid upon me; yea, woe is unto me, if I preach not the gospel!" (1 Cor. 9:16). I do not say that a man cannot be a Christian unless he knows and obeys this impulse. But, at least, we may safely say that he is a very weak and imperfect Christian who does not.

The Universal Obligation

These men were not officials. In these early days the church had a very loose organization. But the fugitives in our narrative seem to have had among them none of the humble office-bearers of primitive times. Neither had they any command or commission from Jerusalem. No one there had given them authority or, as would appear, knew anything of their proceedings. Could there be a more striking illustration of the great truth that whatever varieties of function may be committed to various officers in the church, the work of telling Christ's love to men belongs to everyone who has found it for himself or herself? "This honour have all his saints" (Ps. 149:9).

Whatever may be our differences of opinion as to

church order and offices, they need not interfere with our firm grasp of this truth. "Preaching Christ," in the sense in which that expression is used in the New Testament, implies no one special method of proclaiming the glad tidings. A word written in a letter to a friend, a sentence dropped in casual conversation, a lesson to a child on a mother's lap, or any other way by which, to any listeners, the great story of the cross is told, is as truly—often more truly—preaching Christ as the set discourse that has usurped the name.

We profess to believe in the priesthood of all believers, we are ready enough to assert it in opposition to sacerdotal assumptions. Are we as ready to recognize it as laying a very real responsibility upon us and involving a very practical inference as to our own conduct? We all have the power, therefore we all have the duty. For what purpose did God give us the blessing of knowing Christ ourselves? Not for our own well-being alone, but that through us the blessing might be still farther diffused.

> Heaven doth with us as men with torches do,
> Not light them for themselves.

"God . . . hath shined in our hearts, to give the light of the knowledge of the glory of God in the face of Jesus Christ" (2 Cor. 4:6). Every Christian is solemnly bound to fulfill this Divine intention, and to take heed to the imperative command, "Freely ye have received, freely give" (Matt. 10:8).

The Simple Message

"Preaching the Lord Jesus," says the text—or, more accurately perhaps—preaching Jesus as Lord. The substance then of their message was just this—proclamation of the person and dignity of their Master, the story of the human life of the Man, the story of the divine sacrifice and self-bestowment by which He had bought the right of supreme rule over every heart, and the urging of His claims on all who heard of His love. And this, their message, was but the proclamation of their own personal experience. They had found Jesus for themselves to be lover and Lord, friend and Savior of their souls. The joy they had received they sought to share with these Greeks, worshipers of gods and lords many.

Surely anybody can deliver that message who has had that experience. All have not the gifts that would fit for public speech, but all who have tasted that the Lord is gracious can tell somehow how gracious He is. The first Christian sermon was very short, and it was very efficacious, for it "brought to Jesus" the whole congregation. Here it is: "He first findeth his own brother Simon, and saith unto him, We have found the Messiah" (John 1:41). Surely we can all say that if we have found Him. Surely we shall all long to say it if we are glad that we have found Him, and if we love our brother.

Notice, too, how simple the form as well as the substance of the message. "They *spake*." It was no set address, no formal utterance, but familiar, natural talk to ones and twos, as opportunity offered. The form was so simple that we may say there was none. What we want is that Christian people should speak anyhow. What does the shape of the cup matter? What does it matter whether it be gold or clay? The main thing is that it shall bear the water of life to some thirsty lip. All Christians have to preach as the word is here, that is, to tell the Good News. Their task is to carry a message—no refinement of words is needed for that—arguments are not needed. They have to tell it simply and faithfully as one who only cares to repeat what he has had given to him. They have to tell it confidently, as having proved it true. They have to tell it beseechingly, as loving the souls to whom they bring it. Surely we can all do that if we ourselves are living on Christ and have drunk into His Spirit. Let His mighty salvation, experienced by yourselves, be the substance of your message, and let the form of it be guided by the old words, "And the spirit of the LORD will come upon thee . . . that thou do as occasion serve thee" (1 Sam. 10:6–7).

The Mighty Helper

"The hand of the Lord was with them." The very keynote of this book of the Acts is the work of the ascended

Christ in and for His church. At every turning point in the history, and throughout the whole narratives, forms of speech like this occur bearing witness to the profound conviction of the writer that Christ's active energy was with His servants, and Christ's hand the origin of all their security and of all their success.

So this is a statement of a permanent and universal fact. We do not labor alone. However feeble our hands, that mighty Hand is laid on them to direct their movements and to lend strength to their weakness. It is not our speech that will secure results, but His presence with our words that shall bring it about that even through them a great number shall believe and turn to the Lord. There is our encouragement when we are despondent. There is our rebuke when we are self-confident. There is our stimulus when we are indolent. There is our quietness when we are impatient. If ever we are tempted to think our task heavy, let us not forget that He who set it helps us to do it. From His throne He shares in all our toils, the Lord still, as of old, working with us. If ever we feel that our strength is nothing and that we stand solitary against many foes, let us fall back upon the peace-giving thought that one man against the world, with Christ to help him, is always in the majority. Let us leave issues of our work in His hands, whose hand will guard the seed sown in weakness, whose smile will bless the springing thereof.

How little any of us know what shall become of our poor work under His fostering care! How little these men knew that they were laying the foundations of the great change that was to transform the Christian community from a Jewish sect into a world-embracing church! So is it ever. We know not what we do when simply and humbly we speak His name. The far-reaching issues escape our eyes. Then sow the seed, and He will give it a "body, as it hath pleased him" (1 Cor. 12:18). On earth we may never know the results of our labors. They will be among the surprises of heaven, where many a solitary worker shall claim with wonder as he looks on the hitherto unknown children whom God has given him, "Behold, I was left alone; these, where had they been?" (Isa. 49:21). Then, though our names may have perished from earthly memories—like those of the simple fugitives of Cyprus and Cyrene, who "were the first that ever burst" into the night of heathendom with the torch of the gospel in their hands—they will be written in the Lamb's book of life, and He will confess them in the presence of His Father in heaven.

NOTES

Witnesses

George Campbell Morgan (1863–1945) was the son of
a British Baptist preacher and preached his first sermon
when he was thirteen years old. He had no formal training
for the ministry, but his tireless devotion to the study of
the Bible helped him to become one of the leading Bible
teachers of his day. Rejected by the Methodists, he was
ordained into the Congregational ministry. He was
associated with Dwight L. Moody in the Northfield Bible
conferences and as an itinerant Bible teacher. He is best
known as the pastor of the Westminster Chapel, London
(1904–1917 and 1933–1945). During his second term
there, he had Dr. D. Martyn Lloyd-Jones as his associate.

Morgan published more than sixty books and booklets,
and his sermons are found in *The Westminster Pulpit*
(London: Hodder and Stoughton, 1906–1916). This
sermon was taken from volume 2.

4

WITNESSES

And we are witnesses of these things; and so is the Holy Spirit, whom God hath given to them that obey him (Acts 5:32 ASV).

IN THESE WORDS Peter was the spokesman of the infant church, and he was at once answering a challenge and declaring the solution of a problem. We can appreciate the words at their true value only by remembering the occasion upon which they were spoken. In the context a picture full of life and color is presented to the mind. Two groups of men are seen confronting each other. They constitute a striking contrast. On the one hand are all the men of light and leading and position in Jerusalem, "the high priest . . . and they that were with him . . . and . . . the council . . . and all the senate of the children of Israel" (Acts 5:21). On the other hand are men, not one of them known, save by virtue of their association with Jesus of Nazareth, toiling fishermen of the Galilean Lake with no scholar, no ruler, or no priest in their number. I leave it to your imagination to fill in the details. On the one hand you have the magnificent robing of the priest and his friends, the phylacteries, and the faces with that fine expression that tells of culture and of strong and passionate conviction. On the other hand, you have the homespun and simple garments, the rough and rugged splendor of hard-working men, and all the light gleaming from eyes newly illumined.

The high priest has challenged these men and is strangely perplexed. He has accomplished the death of the troublesome prophet of Nazareth, but a strange story is abroad, told first by the keepers of the grave, and then by the disciples who had been scattered by the crucifixion, that this Jesus is alive and that He has been seen.

51

Of course, he considers it a wild and foolish superstition, but it is having its effect upon both the men who had followed Him in the days of His teaching and those who now heard their preaching. They had flung the ringleaders into prison and in the morning had gathered together that they might deal with them judicially. The message had come that the prison did not contain the men, but that they were in the temple speaking "all the words of this Life" (v. 20).

And now the apostles stand arraigned before priest and rulers. The priest demands of them how they dare continue to preach in the name of Jesus. Peter speaking here, veritably *ex cathedra,* on behalf of the whole church, declared in answer, "We must obey God rather than men. . . . We are witnesses of these things; and so is the Holy Spirit, whom God hath given to them that obey him" (vv. 29, 32).

That was an answer to the challenge of unbelief within a few weeks after Pentecost. It is the answer to the challenge of unbelief today, or we have no answer. In this verse there is declared the function and the force of discipleship, the mission and the method of the church. The function is declared in these words, "We are witnesses of these things." The force is announced in the words, "We . . . and so is the Holy Spirit." The mission of the church is to witness to these things. The method of the church is to act in perpetual cooperation with the Holy Spirit. Wherever the church recognizes this as the function and force of discipleship, as the mission and method of her life, the same results follow as followed in Jerusalem. Wherever the church wanders from this primitive ideal, the early results are wanting. Wherever the church, and all the disciples that constitute the church, remember that the main calling of the church is witness, and that the one and only power of witness is cooperation with the Holy Spirit, then cities are filled with the doctrine and conviction of sin takes hold upon men. The Pentecostal result follows the Pentecostal method.

You will find in this picture, moreover, a contrast of mental attitude. On the one hand we see "the high priest

. . . and [all] they that were with him" (which is the sect of the Sadducees). Who were the Sadducees? I think, perhaps, there is no safer way to answer the question than to take the Bible declaration concerning them. "The Sadducees say that there is no resurrection, neither angel, nor spirit" (23:8). These were the men who challenged the apostles, rationalists, men who denied the supernatural element in religion. Resurrection, angel, spirit—they declared to be superstitions of a bygone age. On the other hand, there is a group of men who testified to the reality of these very things. Said the Sadducee, there is no resurrection. Said the apostles, Christ is risen. Said the Sadducee, there is no angel. Said the apostles, an angel opened the prison doors you shut and let us out. Said the Sadducee, there is no spirit. Said the apostles, we have entered into partnership with the Holy Spirit. It was the beginning of the long struggle between rationalism and Christianity, the conflict between the affirmation of the spiritual as real and the declaration that there is no spirit, but that man lives merely in dust.

Rationalism is still saying there is no resurrection, not even of Christ; there are no angels, they belong to pictures, to art, and to little children's fancies; there is no spirit, the mind is everything. When you have said psychic, you seem to have said the last word of human intellectuality at the present moment.

On the other hand, the church is still saying that Christ rose from among the dead, that angels are all "ministering spirits, sent forth to do service for the sake of them that shall inherit salvation" (Heb. 1:14), that men are essentially spirits, and that there is one Holy Spirit of God. These are the declarations of the church, but how is she to demonstrate the truth of them? The text is answer. "We are witnesses of these things; and so is the Holy Spirit, whom God hath given to them that obey him." Then let us consider these two things, the church's mission, and the method by which she is able to fulfill that mission.

The church's mission is declared in that very simple sentence, "We are witnesses of these things." Where do you suppose Peter put the emphasis when he uttered these words? Let me say, first of all, that I am quite sure he did not lay it upon the personal pronoun. He did not say, "*We* are witnesses of these things." That is where he would have put it before Pentecost, and after Cesarea Philippi. Not so now. The consciousness of personality expressed in the pronoun is lost in the sense of the importance of the witness to be borne. "We are *witnesses*."

I do not think we have yet reached the point of the true emphasis. I think if we had heard Peter that day speak we should have heard him lay the emphasis on *"these things."* What things? "The God of our fathers raised up Jesus, whom ye slew, hanging him on a tree. Him did God exalt with his right hand to be a Prince and a Saviour, to give repentance to Israel, and remission of sins" (Acts 5:30–31). That is the Evangel! Christ is risen. "God . . . raised up Jesus": Christ was crucified. "Whom ye slew, hanging him on a tree": Christ is enthroned. "Him did God exalt to be a Prince and a Saviour": Christ is at work "to give repentance to Israel, and remission of sins." The risen Christ, the crucified Christ, the exalted Christ, the working Christ. "These things." "We are witnesses of these things."

That is the church's mission. The church does not exist to entertain the masses. She is unequal to competition with the theater. The church does not exist to educate the masses. She must be interested in education, but this is not her supreme vocation. The church exists to witness to "these things," the risen Christ, the crucified Christ, the enthroned Christ, the living and working Christ. The world does not want the church. The church cannot save the world. The world wants the things that the church testifies of.

Alas, we have been so anxious about the structure of the lighthouse that we have forgotten often to see that the light is burning. We have been quarreling so busily and with such absolute abandonment concerning forms and garments that we have forgotten the men who wear the garments. We have been more anxious about trappings than about triumph. Find me a man who calls himself a

Christian and does not witness to the risen Christ, the crucified Christ, the exalted Christ, the living, working Christ, and he is of use neither to God nor man. Find me a church where the resurrection light is not shining, where the passion of blood is not proclaimed, and the enthroned Lord is not revealed, and the working Lord is not felt. It is a tomb, an insult to God and to man. "These things," that is the church's business. "We are witnesses of these things."

Yet let us think of the word "witnesses." A witness is more than a man who talks. Indeed a man may talk and never witness in the New Testament sense of the word. It has been repeatedly pointed out that the word here translated, and translated uniformly throughout the New Testament "witness," is a Greek word that we have anglicized into our word "martyr": "We are [martyrs] of these things." What is a martyr? We have come to use the word of such as seal their testimony with their blood. It is a beautiful word for such. When we speak of the "noble army of martyrs," who through flame and fire, through blood and suffering, proved their loyalty to Christ, let us remember that the fires did not make them martyrs. The fires did but reveal them to be martyrs. They were martyrs before the fires were lit, or they would never have submitted to them. Every day of fiery persecution has been a day when martyrs have been revealed.

What, then, is a martyr? He is a confessor. A martyr is one who is first convinced of truth. He then yields his life to the claims of the truth of which he is convinced and, therefore, is changed by the truth that he believes and to which he has yielded himself. So that, finally, a martyr is a specimen, an evidence, a sample, a credential, a proof, a witness. We are the credentials of these things. We are the proof of these things. We say Jesus is risen from the dead. We say the risen Christ is the self-same Christ who was crucified. We say this Christ is exalted by God. We say this Christ is at work giving repentance and remission of sins. How are we going to prove these things? We are evidences. We prove the accuracy of our doctrine by the transformation of our lives.

The apostle did not merely mean, as he stood in the presence of that august company of rulers and priests, that they bore testimony in words, that they were prepared to argue. He meant rather to say, "You deny the resurrection. You deny the value we declare to have been created by the dying of this Christ whom you slew. You deny that Jesus of Nazareth is on the throne of God. You deny that He is alive and working in Jerusalem!" Go back and think of us as we were and behold us as we are. We are what we are by virtue of the things we declare. It is by the risen Christ who was crucified, is exalted, and is at work that we are what we are. Rationalism has no right to deny the accuracy of the supernatural claims of Christ until it can account for the wonders wrought in men and women who by Christianity have been changed from all that is base to everything that is noble, from being slaves to sin into being bond slaves of Christ, from being men consumed by lust and passion to men consumed by zeal for the salvation of men and for the glory of God.

That is the supreme value of my text as it reveals the work of the church. The church confronts the age with living witnesses. If she has none, she is useless. If she has none, she has no argument. If she is not able to present to the age in all its rationalism and unbelief men and women changed, remade, she has no argument to which the age will listen. Such a declaration as that reacts upon the heart and conscience of every Christian man or woman, or ought so to do. Am I a witness? I do not mean am I a preacher. Unless behind the preaching of my lips there is the testimony of my life, my preaching is blasphemy and impertinence. Unless my own life is changed and transformed and transfigured, a revelation of the fact of the risen, crucified, exalted, working Christ, my preaching is as "sounding brass or a clanging cymbal" (1 Cor. 13:1). So with all of us. Any recitation of creed is blasphemy unless the creed is alive in conduct. Your affirmation of the truth of the Christian facts is impertinence unless in the very fiber of your personality these things are wrought out and are shining through in revelation upon the age. "We are witnesses of these things."

I get back at last to the personal pronoun. "*We* are witnesses of these things." Who were they? As I have said, none of them counted at all by any of the ordinary standards of human measurement. They were fishermen. Do you not think that term was often used of them disdainfully in those days? These Galilean fishermen! Yet they were witnesses of such things as made them makers of empire, and revolutionaries who turned the world upside down! Not they, but the things through them. The very simplest of the men who answered the claims of the things, and became transformed thereby, became also a force. There is no man here so weak but that if these things are by him believed, and he by them is changed, he becomes appointed a witness in apostolic succession, in Christly fellowship, in actual cooperation with God, a part of the divine movement for bruising the head of the enemy and destroying the works of the Devil, and bringing in the triumph of righteousness.

They were poor Galilean fishermen, of no account, of no value in themselves, but they live in the imagination of this age while the priests are remembered by their garments and their phylacteries and their folly.

Yes, but how did they do it? "We are witnesses of these things; and so is the Holy Spirit, whom God hath given to them that obey him." The Spirit is witness of the things of Christ. Jesus before He left His disciples instructed them concerning the days of His absence and said of the Spirit, "the [Paraclete] . . . shall teach you all things, and bring to your remembrance all that I said unto you. . . . He shall bear witness of me. . . . He shall glorify me" (John 14:26; 15:26; 16:14). He declared that the mission of the Holy Spirit would be the interpretation of Himself. For the sake of the truth being remembered let me try to condense that great doctrine of the Spirit into two of the simplest of all sentences, so simple that there will be the same words in both but differently arranged for the revelation of a different value.

> The Holy Spirit witnesses of Jesus only.
> Only the Holy Spirit witnesses of Jesus.

Think of the first. The Holy Spirit witnesses of Jesus only. How we forget it as Christian people! Christian people constantly pray for the coming of the Holy Spirit and wait for His coming. In their minds there seems to be the idea that when the Spirit comes to them in fullness they will be conscious of the Spirit. There is no evidence of any such teaching in Scripture. If the Spirit come to us in all fullness, He will make us conscious, not of Himself, but of Christ. "He shall not speak from himself. . . . He shall take of mine, and shall declare it unto you," said Christ (16:13–14).

I would like to stay with that in all tenderness because I think there are sincere souls being misled by their own thinking in this regard. It is not long since a young man came to me and said, I do not quite understand my relationship to Christ. I am a little puzzled by it. I have long been praying for the fullness of the Spirit and waiting for it and longing for it and earnestly desiring it. I have heard of others who have received it, but it does not come to me. I began to talk to him, and I found that he thought when the Spirit came in fullness there would be a flash of light and glory, a thrill and enthusiasm, and consciousness of fire and of the Holy Spirit. It is not so. All the while, through the days, weeks, months of his sincere seeking, this thing had been happening in his experience, Christ was becoming more precious than He was, far more real! The Spirit was there doing His work, unveiling Christ, yet this man did not recognize that the Spirit was fulfilling His one great function. The Spirit comes to witness to Jesus only. Once, tongues of fire and a mighty rushing wind, evidence to the senses of the coming of the Spirit. From that moment, straight on through generations, He has hidden Himself. The Spirit comes to reveal Jesus only. He has no other message, no other work than the unveiling of the face of Christ, in which we see the unveiling of the face of God.

Take my other sentence for a moment and consider it. Only the Holy Spirit witnesses of Jesus. Does this seem to contradict Peter's declaration, "We are witnesses"? By no means. How did they become witnesses? In the hour when they crowned Jesus Lord. Listen, "No man can say, Jesus is Lord, but in the Holy Spirit" (1 Cor. 12:3). I cannot make you call Him Lord. I can speak of His lordship, of the perfection of His life, of the passion of His death, of the power of His resurrection, of the program of His reign, and you will hear it all and intellectually consent to the fact that He is Lord. But you never can look into His face and say, "Lord," save as the Spirit of God has unveiled His glory and captured your heart. It is the Spirit of God who first reveals to the soul the lordship of Jesus. So these men became witnesses because on the day of Pentecost they had seen Christ as they had never seen Him before. Think of it. They had looked at Christ for three years and had never, never seen Him. They had felt the touch of His human hand and never, never found Him. When the day of Pentecost came and the Spirit came as fire and power, they saw Him and became witnesses. Have you seen Him? It is only by the Spirit's unveiling of the face of Christ that He is ever seen, or that men become His witnesses.

When once the Lord has been seen and crowned there is a progressive operation of the Spirit in the life of the believer. The Spirit reveals the Christ to you in some new aspect as you read His Word, as you meditate upon Him. The moment you see Christ in some new glory, that vision makes a demand upon you. What are you going to do with it? Answer it, obey it, and the Spirit realizes in you the thing you have seen in Christ. Disobey it, and the Spirit has no other message to you until you return to that point of disobedience and have become obedient.

I wonder if you will be patient if for a moment I pass from advocacy to witnessing. I remember with clear distinctness how more than twenty years ago I read a passage in Matthew's gospel that I had read hundreds of times, but in that moment it flamed and burned before my eyes. It was this, "When He saw the multitudes, he was moved with compassion" (Matt. 9:36). I cannot give you what I saw. No man can pass these visions on. You must only hear me patiently, for the lonely vision is for the lonely soul. In that moment to which my own memory goes back, and which lives with me now, I saw the very heart of the Son of God. I saw that compassion as I had never known it, although I had been saved by it.

A vision like that is not merely an illumination of the intellect for the entertainment or delight of the soul that sees it. It is a clarion call, a trumpet blast! It said to me: If you are His and you share His life, you must answer His passion and be willing to follow Him in service that is sacrificial service. Now, let me drop the personal. Granted that any man see that as I saw it that night, two pathways open out before him. It is the Spirit's unveiling of the compassion of Christ to the soul. What will the man do who sees it? He can stifle it, admire it merely, and never answer it until the vision dim and die away, and the Spirit will have no more to say to him. Or he can answer it, give himself to sacrificial service, be willing to die in service, and then the Spirit will lead him further on to higher heights and deeper depths. That is but one illustration.

The Spirit is always unveiling Christ. Your responsibility and mine, if we would cooperate with Him in witness, is that we obey when He speaks. When Christ is seen in a new light, the light is calling you to obey its claim. Answer it and you will become the thing you have seen. Deny it and you will sink to lower levels. This is His method, line upon line, here a little and there a little, grace for grace, beauty after beauty.

People, you have never seen Christ, nor have I. I have seen something of Him, like a blind man waking to his first vision I have seen men as trees walking. I have seen more and more of the beauty of my Lord as the Spirit has unveiled Him, but I have never seen all the glory. I could not bear it yet. So little by little the Spirit patiently leads us on. Our responsibility is that when light comes we walk in it. When the trumpet call of truth sounds in our souls we must answer it. The Spirit's office—and He never fails—is to reveal Christ. Our duty is to answer the revelation. When we do so, the Spirit becomes more than illumination, He becomes dynamic and makes us that which we obey.

Soul of mine, answer the light. Obey the Spirit. Do not resist, do not grieve, do not quench the Spirit, and you, even you, poor broken man of the dust, shall be made like Him. What is heaven, I pray you tell? Seeing Him and being like Him. To that goal the Spirit leads.

Now hear me as I say this in conclusion. It is when I act in cooperation with this Spirit who reveals Jesus only, who only reveals Jesus, that I become His witness. That brings me back to the emphasis I placed a few moments ago upon the word "witness." I pray you now place the emphasis upon "witness" by linking it with that other Witness. The Spirit witnessing in me, I become the instrument through which the Spirit witnesses to the world. Where? Anywhere. When? Whenever. God deliver us from the heresy of ever imagining that we witness only when we are in the pulpit and from the heresy of imagining that what the world wants is more preaching. Preaching is of no use save as it makes living witnesses. How have I failed, how awfully have I failed, God have mercy upon me, if I have simply held you and interested you for this hour. But if I have sent you back to your office tomorrow, back to your store, back to your home, back to your place in the government to be more like Christ, I have hastened the coming of the day of God. I have done something to bring the kingdom in. He gave some apostles, some prophets, some evangelists, some pastors and teachers—to preach men to heaven? No, no! What, then? To perfect the saints to the work of ministering.

The truth I preach is of value in the ultimate issue only as it is incarnate in the lives of the men who listen. London is perishing for lack of living witnesses. The world awaits the evangel of transformed, transfigured lives. Will you be a witness? You say, How can I? The answer is in the text, "the Holy Spirit, whom God hath given to them that obey him." You have looked into the face of the Lord Christ. Intellectually, you have seen Him and have acknowledged that He is Lord. Crown Him. Submit to Him. Trust Him. Do it with something of heroism, I beseech you. Do it with something of daring, I implore you. The influence of the church is sadly hindered, the world is sadly hindered by dilettante discipleship. Crown Christ. Obey Him. Cut the last shore rope that binds you to the old life. In the moment that you crown Him the Holy Spirit will baptize you into unity of life with Him, and you will become His witness.

NOTES

The Worldwide Gospel

George H. Morrison (1866–1928) assisted the great Alexander Whyte in Edinburgh, pastored two churches, and then became pastor in 1902 of the distinguished Wellington Church on University Avenue in Glasgow, Scotland. His preaching drew great crowds; in fact, people had to line up an hour before the services to be sure to get seats in the large auditorium. Morrison was a master of imagination in preaching, yet his messages are solidly biblical.

From his many published volumes of sermons, I have chosen this message, found in *The World-Wide Gospel,* published in 1933 by Hodder and Stoughton, London.

George H. Morrison

5

THE WORLDWIDE GOSPEL

Go ye into all the world, and preach the gospel to every creature (Mark 16:15).

THERE ARE TWO DIRECTIONS in which the sway of Jesus is without any parallel in human history. The one of them is that of depth; the other is that of breadth. All great movements may be judged extensively, that is, by the area that they cover. Or, on the other hand, they may be judged intensively by their power of influence over the individual. In both respects the gospel of our Lord stands quite alone upon the page of history—in its depth and in its breadth it is unequaled.

The one name for the followers of Socrates was the name of disciple, or of learner. That name was often on the lips of Christ and is familiar on the gospel page. But it is very significant that, as the days went by and men perceived all that they owed to Christ, the name of disciple (for all its tender memories) gave place to that of servant or slave. That indicates with what a perfect mastery Jesus Christ controls the individual. His influence reaches to the depths of being, and possesses every power and every passion.

Yet not less notable than that complete control is the area over which it is to reach: "Go ye into all the world, and preach the gospel to every creature." The two remarkable things about the gospel are that it is deep as life and is wide as all the world. It is a message of redeeming power for the whole man. It is a message of redeeming power for every man. And on that latter subject I wish to speak today: on the worldwide message of the gospel. First, let us look at it in its conception; next, in its accomplishment; and, lastly, in its obligation.

The Conception

First, then, the worldwide message of the gospel, viewed in the light of its conception: "Go ye into all the world, and preach the gospel to every creature." These words were uttered by the risen Lord when the agony of Calvary was over. It was when He was soon to leave His own that He commanded them to go into the world. It has been argued hence that this idea was only present with Jesus at the end. Had He succeeded in converting Israel, this destiny would never have emerged. It was His failure, we are told, with His own people, and the reaction of a brave spirit from that failure, that led Him to think that all might not be lost though Israel refused Him for its King. In other words, it has been argued that the worldwide message was an afterthought. It was not part—if I may put it so—of the original program of the Christ. It was the child of disappointed hope born of His failure with unbelieving Israel; the last dream, if not the last infirmity, of a noble mind.

Now, brethren, there are certain of Christ's thoughts of which you can trace the development. You can see them forming with the passing days into the fullness of our Christian heritage. But the thought of the worldwide mission of the gospel can never be included in that number, for from the first hour of His public ministry it was present to the mind of Christ.

Think, for instance, of that mysterious hour when Christ was tempted in the wilderness. The last temptation was the sorest one, and you recall what that last temptation was: "Again, the devil taketh him up into an exceeding high mountain, and showeth him all the kingdoms of the world, and the glory of them; and saith unto him, All these things will I give thee, if thou wilt fall down and worship me" (Matt. 4:8–9). Now, how do our bitterest temptations reach us? They reach us along the line of our desires. They offer us immediately, and in forbidden ways, the things we covet and hunger for and crave for. And if in the desert the bitterest temptation was couched in dreams of universal empire, you may be sure that universal empire was the ruling passion in the

Savior's heart. It was not in the sovereignty that the temptation lay. It was in the way suggested to achieve the sovereignty. It was in the prompting to take the nearest road instead of the bloodstained path that led by Calvary. And the very fact that Christ was tempted so when he was fresh from His mother's home at Nazareth shows us that even then there burned within Him the hope and the vision of a worldwide kingdom.

Or, again, take the Sermon on the Mount, which is the charter and the program of His kingdom. That it was spoken early in His ministry is not a matter open to dispute. Well, now, in Psalm 37 you read that the meek shall inherit the land. It is not so translated in our version, but that is the only meaning of the Hebrew. The psalmist is thinking of the land of Palestine, and thinking of nothing but the land of Palestine. He looks for a day when pride shall disappear, and every dweller in the land to be lowly. And now comes Christ, and He strikes out that word "land." In its stead He places the word "earth"— "Blessed are the meek: for they shall inherit the earth" (Matt. 5:5)—thus, the bounds of Palestine have been submerged. And then, as if to confirm that spacious thought, He says to those who follow Him, "Ye are the salt of the earth. . . . Ye are the light of the world" (vv. 13–14). Clearly, then, at the outset of His ministry our Lord had His eyes fixed upon the world. The worldwide mission of His gospel message was not the late-born child of disappointment. In all its grandeur it possessed His heart when first He opened His lips upon the hill, and it abode with Him unaltered until the end when He said, "Go ye into all the world."

Now, there are two features in this conception to which I desire to direct your thoughts, and the first is its overwhelming boldness. If you would but reflect for a moment on the facts and on the circumstances that surround the facts, there is not one of you but would be amazed at the unparalleled boldness of the Lord. We have read of an Alexander conquering the world and then weeping that there were not other worlds to conquer. But Alexander was born in a king's estate and had a mighty army to obey him. We have read of Napoleon, with his vast ambition and his dreams of a mighty empire in the East, but Napoleon also had his hardy veterans, and his ambition rose with his success. How different from all this is Jesus Christ, who had not a single sword to back His claims, and who, in the quiet glory of His faith, believed in His worldwide empire from the first. Had He been born in Rome of Latin ancestry we might have better understood His outlook. For Rome was stretching her power into far distances and widening the horizon of her children. But Jesus Christ was born after the flesh, of the narrowest and most exclusive race that ever lived. Yet out of the heart of that most jealous heritage He looked with equal eyes upon the whole world. In every land His gospel would be preached. In every tongue His name would be proclaimed. "Heaven and earth shall pass away, but my words shall not pass away" (Matt. 24:35; Mark 13:31; Luke 21:33). Who was He to make these mighty claims? He was the meek and lowly man of Nazareth whose mother had never heard the name of Plato and whose brethren moved about a village street.

Note, too, in what a natural way our Savior talked about His worldwide mission. He did not dwell on it as one might dwell on something stupendous that was overwhelming Him. But He spoke of it as quietly and simply as you and I might talk about our work, without the slightest trace of any feeling that He had taken on Him a task that was too great. Think of Him as He sat in Simon's house when the woman broke the alabaster box. "She hath poured this ointment on my body, she did it for my burial," He said (Matt. 26:12). And then He added, in the same quiet voice, that "wheresoever this gospel shall be preached in the whole world, there shall also this, that this woman hath done, be told for a memorial of her" (v. 13). It is easy to say that the world to Jesus must have meant far less than it means today for us. I question if it did not mean far more than it does now, when you can mail to Africa. But at least to one who had seen the Roman soldiers drafted from strange regions of the empire to one who had moved amid the crowds at Passover, drawn from the towns and cities of far lands, there must always have been a grandeur and a breadth in the conception of a worldwide mission.

The other feature is its originality. I question if we think enough on that. The program of a universal empire was as original as it was daring. There was nothing like it in the Jewish creed. The Jewish religion was rigidly exclusive. There was nothing like it in the pagan world, where religion and the state were almost one. It was a thought transcendently original, and original because it was divine, that now there was to be neither Jew nor Greek, barbarian nor Scythian, bond nor free. It is not from particular promises that we learn the originality of Jesus. There is scarcely a beatitude whose germ, at any rate, you may not find in a page of the Old Testament. Christ is most deeply indebted to the past, and to those who sang and sorrowed in the past, but it is His glory that sets the past in a light that never was on land or sea.

Take, for example, the thought of the kingdom of heaven, an expression that was often on His lips. It was a word familiar to the Jews, and its coming was proclaimed by John the Baptist. Yet between the kingdom of Jewish aspiration and the kingdom as announced by Jesus Christ, there was a world of spiritual difference. The one was earthly, and the other heavenly. The one was national, and the other universal. The one had its seat and center in Jerusalem; the other had its bond of unity in Christ. The marching order of the one was this, "Come ye, and worship in the holy temple," while these were the marching orders of the other, "Go ye into all the world, and preach the gospel." Remember, then, that we owe to Jesus Christ our familiar thought of a worldwide religion. It is one of the grandest and most sublime ideas that has ever been granted to the human race. And not to Greeks do we owe it, nor to Rome. We owe it to Jesus Christ our Savior to whom it was given, not from the past of Israel, but from the Father with whom He was one.

The Accomplishment

In the second place, let us view this worldwide mission in the light of its accomplishment. Now it is one thing to cherish great ideas, and quite another to see these ideas fulfilled. We know what a gulf there is between a great conception and its actual achievement upon the stage of history. Sometimes the great idea proves impracticable and takes its place among Utopian dreams. Sometimes, in contact with the rude reality, it is so crushed and bruised that none would recognize it.

I may recall to your memory two great conceptions that have fared in these two ways in history. One of the best-known works of Plato the philosopher is the treatise that pictures his ideal Republic. It is a pattern of what a state should be when ruled by the wisest and for the wisest ends. Yet this—this kingdom of heaven of philosophy—has had so little power in touch with fact that to this day, in spite of its moral grandeur, it is an impracticable and insubstantial dream.

On the other hand, in the time of the French Revolution, there rose the conception of an ideal kingdom. Its watchwords were *liberty, equality,* and *fraternity,* and it was to inaugurate a golden age. So big with promise did that conception seem, and so like to be the dawn of the millennium, that for enthusiasts and generous hearts "bliss was it in that dawn to be alive." I need hardly tell you what actually happened—how hopes were dashed and aspirations shattered. The prisons were crowded, guillotines were busy, and the streets ran red with the blood of slaughtered men. Here was a great conception of a kingdom within whose bounds there would be peace and liberty; yet, in actual contact with the brutal fact, it turned itself into a scene of carnage.

Now think, in contradistinction from all this, of the worldwide kingdom announced by Jesus Christ. Slowly and silently it made its way from nation to nation and from land to land. It was no impracticable and insubstantial dream, as could be witnessed by a thousand lives. In the peace and power that it brought it was true to the first design of its one Lord. As an actual fact, from the moment of its birth the gospel has been steadily advancing. It has broken down the barriers of class; it has survived the changes of the centuries. Nations have risen and perished in the world since Jesus moved along the ways of Galilee. Ancient empires have crumbled into dust and new continents have swung within our ken, but still the gospel message is proclaimed, still men are going forth with its glad news, still Christ is proving Himself in distant lands the wisdom and the power of God.

Now, not only is this an actual fact, but we must remember it is also a unique fact. There is not another religion in the world of which the same assertion can be made. If you can point to any other faith that has traveled far from the region of its birth, then one might think, on purely natural grounds, to explain the wonderful spread of Christianity. But such a faith is nowhere to be found in all the great historical regions, though some of them have had the aid of allies that Christianity would scorn to own.

Think, for example, of Muhammadanism. With its consecration of sensual indulgence, with its sword of steel, and with its heaven of sense, well fitted might it seem to win the world. Yet Muhammadanism has never touched the West. And, however powerful with its own people, it has never succeeded in laying its hands on peoples who are remote from its first home. Or think of Buddhism, with its so gentle touch and all the soothing of its voice for weary men, for two thousand years and more its spell has lain on the unnumbered millions of the East. Yet, in all these centuries, it has never crossed the boundary that separates the Orient from the Occident, never wooed the nations of the West with its dreamy gospel of despair.

Now, with both these contrast the Christian gospel. It was cradled in a little Eastern land, and within a hundred years it was in Spain. Then within a hundred years it was in Scotland. Now, when but eighteen centuries are gone, in the remotest East and furthest West men, on fire with love for Jesus Christ, are preaching the glad news of the Evangel. There is nothing like this in the history of the nations; nothing like it in the story of religion. It is unparalleled; it is unique. I do not hesitate to say it is divine. The steady progress of the Christian faith for him who has eyes to see and ears to hear is one of the strongest of all arguments for the divinity of Jesus Christ.

And this impression is singularly deepened when we think of the forces allied against the gospel. It had against it the power of the state, and, still more powerful, the heart of man. I shall not dwell upon persecutions that fell with such terrific force upon the church. Other religions have been persecuted too, and they, like the gospel of Jesus, have survived. Far more remarkable than that survival from the bitter persecution of the state is its survival from these deadlier evils that lay in their infancy on its own bosom. When I think of the heresies that rent the early church—of her gradual decline from spirituality, of the superstition of the Middle Ages, and the widespread skepticism it engendered—and how the church has been rent into divisions, and how Protestant and Catholic stand apart, to me it is wonderful that men should ever dream now of carrying the gospel to the world.

As a matter of fact, not only do they dream it, every day they actually do it. Never before, in all the Christian centuries, has there been such eagerness to evangelize the world. And, when you think of the story of the past, with all its division and all its degradation, that glowing zeal of the Christian church today is a mighty witness to the living Christ. Every power that could wreck the gospel has been brought to bear on it since it was born. It has been persecuted, ridiculed, degraded. It has been wounded by foes and by its friends. And yet today what about Livingstonia, India, Manchuria, and Old Calabar? Why, if Christ be not alive, I tell you that all that is inexplicable. I pity with all my heart the man or woman who says he does not believe in foreign missions. He is shutting his heart to such a splendid proof of the divinity of Jesus Christ. "Go ye into all the world, and preach the gospel to every creature," and men are doing it to this very hour. To me, knowing the past, that is inexplicable unless the speaker was the Son of God.

The Obligation

And now, in closing and in a word or two, this worldwide mission in its obligation. And, first, it is the duty of us all to realize what we owe to this command, "Go ye into all the world, and preach." Why, that has been the charter of our liberty. Without it there would have been no gospel here. And without the gospel, who can picture Britain? I hear of some who believe in home missions, but have no interest in foreign missions. That attitude, I believe, is often due to lack of imagination rather than of heart. But remember, if a thousand years ago the church had taken a standpoint of that kind, we would still have been living in a heathen Britain and without a single hope in Jesus Christ. It is to the foreign missions of the past that Britain owes her highest life today. It is to men who left their home and country that we are indebted for the Christian faith. In spite of all that disgraces our profession and all the indifference that fills our land, no patriot has ever done for Britain a thousandth part of what has been done by Christ.

It is not fair to judge of foreign missions merely by what you see or hear today. Even that, when it is rightly read, is full of argument and inspiration. The foreign missions are as old as Christendom. It is they that started Europe on her course, and rightly to know the worth of foreign missions you must include that story of the past. But not alone must we strive to realize all that the worldwide faith has done for us. Each one of us must make the text our own if we are truly disciples of the Lord. To some here there has come the call to go abroad, and they have opened their hearts to hear that call. God grant that even today there may be others who will be drawn to dedicate their lives to this great service. But every one of us, whether old or young, can play his part in this unequaled labor and help on, more powerfully than we know, the promised evangelization of the world.

Read, I pray you, with attention the story of that service in our missionary journals. Take an intelligent interest in the matter, as I know so many of you already do. Give it a large place in daily prayer and be not content with general petitions, but, with a mind enriched by information, intercede for particular localities. It is in such ways that we can take our place, though we may not stand in the forefront of the battle. By prayer, by interest, by thoughtful giving, we can help the worldwide triumph of the gospel. For that great victory will surely come when the knowledge of Christ shall cover the whole earth, and happy shall he be who, in that crowning hour, shall be found to have hastened on its coming.

NOTES

The Constraining Love of Christ

John Henry Jowett (1864–1923) was known as "the greatest preacher in the English-speaking world." He was born in Yorkshire, England. He was ordained into the Congregational ministry, and his second pastorate was at the famous Carr's Lane Church, Birmingham, where he followed the eminent Dr. Robert W. Dale. From 1911 to 1918, he pastored the Fifth Avenue Presbyterian Church, New York City; from 1918 to 1923, he ministered at Westminster Chapel, London, succeeding G. Campbell Morgan. He wrote many books of devotional messages and sermons.

This message was taken from the *Mundesley Bible Conference Report, 1915,* published by Morgan and Scott, London.

John Henry Jowett

6

THE CONSTRAINING LOVE OF CHRIST

The love of Christ constraineth us (2 Corinthians 5:14).

"CONSTRAINETH!" What is the weight and content of the word? What is its strength and quality and color? The word that Paul uses concerning the love of Christ is one of great power and intensity. In common discourse it throbbed with energy. Its usage in other relationships in the New Testament reveals its force and tenacity. Let us glance at one or two of these usages so that we may return to our text with richer powers of interpretation.

Usages of the Word "Constraineth"

Here is one: "They were *taken* with great fear" (Luke 8:37). Let the imagination work upon the phrase. We know how mighty is the tyranny of fear, and how it lays its enslaving hand upon all the powers of body, mind, and soul. And yet the word that is used to express the dominion of a fear is used by the apostle Paul to express the hold upon him of the love of Christ. Just as some souls are possessed and enslaved by fear, Paul was possessed and enslaved by love. "The love of God constraineth me."

Here is another New Testament usage of the word: "The multitude *throng* thee" (Luke 8:45). The very word that is here translated "throng" lends its color and intensity to the word of my text: "The multitude throng thee." Have you ever been caught by the grip and the current of a thronging multitude?

I can vividly recall an experience I had as a boy when I went to hear a great and famous statesman address a meeting of his countrymen in the town of Bradford. It was before the saving expedient of the line had been devised, and the crowd gathered in one dense and solid mass about the door. And when the door was opened the crowd moved as a packed unit. Again and again I was lifted bodily off my feet and carried forward by the force of the multitude in the one direction of the open door. "The multitude throng thee!" And it is that word "throng," descriptive of that mass movement—the carrying of the unit in the tendency of the crowd—that the apostle uses to describe the effect upon him of the love of Christ. "The love of Christ [throngs] me"—it gets around my soul with all the mass and momentum of a great crowd. It carries me off my feet, and it bears me onward and forward in the gracious purpose of my God. "The love of Christ [throngs] me!" The love of Christ constraineth me.

Let me give you still another New Testament use of the word, for I am sure it is well worthwhile to enrich our conception of its significance. Here it is: "The men that *held* Jesus mocked Him" (Luke 22:63).

Just try to imagine the hold these brutal men had on Jesus Christ. He was their prisoner. The heavy hand of arrest was upon Him. They would not let Him go. And it is that usage, the conception of a strong and arresting hand gripping a prisoner, that the apostle applies to the hold that the love of Christ has upon him. It arrests him. It grips him. It holds him prisoner. "O love that wilt not let me go!" "The love of Christ constraineth me! " He was its prisoner, held in its strong and most authoritative hand.

These are a few of the manifold significances of this most wealthy word, which the apostle uses to describe his conception and experience of the love of Christ. That love possesses him with the pervasiveness of a great fear. The love of Christ bears him forward with the irresistible momentum of a vast crowd. The love of Christ holds him prisoner in the strong arresting grip of a detaining band. It is the holding of a great fear; it is the thronging of a great crowd; it is a grip that holds him captive. "The love of Christ constraineth me."

Now to a certain degree this is true of all love. I suppose every kind of love is in its own degree endowed with these forces of constraint. That is to say, every form of true love has dynamic. Indeed, I think it might be a truer way of putting it to say that every form of true love is dynamic. It has power because it is power. Think of the constraining power of a parent's love for a child. What constraining power there is in it, constraining to be and to do and to live and to die! The love of a mother for her child possesses her, throngs her, grips her, holds her in a mighty, yet delicately tender constraint.

I have been lately reading the life of the principal of my old college, at Mansfield, Dr. Fairbairn, and I was deeply touched by a sentence in a letter he wrote to his oldest son when the lad was just deciding upon his career.

> When you were a little child I often thought how willingly I would consent to be nothing and do nothing in the world if I could only make you a good man! And I feel so still, anxious only to see you one who could serve your God and your kind! If you do that, I shall be happy to be remembered only as your father.

It is an intensely gracious word! There is a depth of love glowing in that quiet sentence that no one can measure. It was a love that constrained that great and noble soul to woo even obscurity if only his son might be honored and blessed. The love of child constrained him.

You will find the same dynamic of constraint in a passionate patriotism. We are learning, as perhaps we have never learned before in our time, what love of country will constrain men and women to do. How it arrests them, grips them, holds them prisoner, throngs them, and carries them off their feet—carries them into ways of pain and hardship and endurance and sacrifice. I say that patriotism, love of country, has this outstanding dynamic. It is possessed with a quenchless inspiration that dares to face the most menacing antagonism, and to be serene and mighty even in the imminent approach of death. The love of country "constraineth" me.

But here we have the supreme application of the great word—this fine, muscular, masculine word in Paul's application of it—to the hold of the love of the Lord Jesus in his soul. "The love of Christ constraineth me." What does he mean? Does he mean that the constraint was to be found in Christ's love for him, or was the constraint to be found in his love for Christ? Did Paul's love for his great Savior hold him, or did the love of the great Savior hold him, in its grip? Surely we cannot divide the two. Surely the love is inclusive of both. Christ's love for him awakened his love for Christ. The divine fire kindled the flame of sacred love on the mean altar of his heart. The divine love came to him like the breath of the spring. There was a gracious quickening and the birth of spiritual beauty, and there ascended to the Lord the fragrant incense of a responsive love. "We love him, because he first loved us" (1 John 4:19). And therefore I think we cannot rightly divide the two.

But even thus, while I think of this constraining love as a mingling of two loves, yet in the mingling it was the Savior's love that was altogether preeminent—the initial love, the love that generated love, the love that ministered when there was only the unlovely to love, the love that was loving when there was no response, loving when apparently there was nothing to love. How the apostle exults in the wonderful love of his Lord! You cannot get away from the rapture of it in any one of his letters. If you had been with him for an hour he would have led you into the sunshine of his Savior's love. You know the apostle Paul would at any time stop an argument to sing a doxology. That makes Paul so difficult to read. He would argue and argue and, then in the midst of his reasonings, catch a glimpse of what he calls "the unsearchable riches of Christ" (Eph. 3:8). Then he would begin to sing what I have called his doxology on the theme of his Redeemer's love. His soul just bursts out in rapture like the spontaneous songs of happy birds.

[He] loved me, and gave himself for me (Gal. 2:20).

His great love wherewith he loved us (Eph. 2:4).

Christ also hath loved us, and hath given himself for us an offering and a sacrifice to God (Eph. 5:2).

Who shall separate us from the love of Christ? (Rom. 8:35).

And this is the unquenchable ambition of the great apostle. When in the epistle to the Philippians he is gathering up and converging his aspirations and ambitions into one, they are focused in his magnificent intensity, "To know the love of Christ which passeth knowledge" (Eph. 3:19). And therefore I say that this is the unquenchable ambition and aspiration of the great apostle. The love of Christ held him, took him, thronged him, constrained him, and in the Beulah land of his soul all the birds were singing night and day.

Now, what had the love of Christ done for him? It had made him a "new man" (Eph. 4:24; Col. 3:10). That is the apostle's claim. That is not a big word for a little thing; it is an altogether inadequate word for an altogether ineffable thing. The love of Christ had made this man into another man. Paul does not merely mean that a crooked thing had been made straight; he does not mean that crooked habits had been untwisted into rectitude. He means that the vital stuff and substance of his being had been transformed.

I do not know any theologian of the last generation who held to that with such splendid and positive dogmatism as my great predecessor at Carr's Lane, Dr. Dale. Whenever he spoke about the effective and efficient and saving work of the Lord Jesus, it was not a mere quickening process, but the impartation actually of new life. I have heard Dale say, and he said in his books the same thing again and again, that when the Lord Jesus Christ lays hold of a man and begins His saving work upon that man, he receives a new life as literally and as positively as he received life in his mother's womb. A new man! A new creation! It is the apostle's own words, "If any man be in Christ, he is a new creature" (2 Cor. 5:17). The love of Christ had given Paul a new beginning. He had been created a "new man in Christ Jesus." Christ had taken Paul's guilt and died for it. "Christ . . . loved me and gave Himself for me." Christ had taken Paul's forgiven soul and quickened it with the impartation of His own life. Christ had died for him. Christ now lived for him. "Old things are passed away, behold, all things are become new" (v. 17). And the love of Christ had done it all—"all to Him I owe."

Now let us never be so unwise as to call this page of apostolic witness a remote and old-world story that has no living relationship to our own day. When I quote a great theologian like Dr. Dale, a great saint like Dale, I am only rereading the experience and teaching of the apostle Paul. And when we read a page like that out of apostolic history, never let us assume for a moment that it belongs to effete worn-out days. We are speaking of a man's experience of miracles of that kind of grace when, as I have said, the very substance and stuff of a man's soul are absolutely transformed.

Let me take one of the very latest of my own experiences, concerning a man whom I have known for twenty years, and whom I have been mercifully privileged to lead into the kingdom of light and joy and peace. He is a man of real ability. His powers pushed all difficulties aside, just as Samson snapped the withes that bound him, and he came into great wealth and prosperity. But as his luxury grew, the animal grew until the animal got the throne, and he was sunk into unutterable profanity and beasthood. Yes, the mark of the beast was upon him. You could read it in his forehead. And, then, by an apparent accident, but by a real Providence, he crossed the seas, and there in the depths of shameful need he met his Lord. And no words of mine can tell you what the love of Christ has done for him. None but this loved one knows. But the rapture of Paul is in his soul, and his life is gloriously illumined with the radiant presence of his Lord. He was brought into an experience like that of Catherine of Sienna or David Brainerd or Horace Bushnell, in the most intimate, constraining love of those great souls. My friend had the very rapture of the apostle Paul in his spirit, and his life is gloriously irradiated and the mark of the beast wiped out by the indwelling presence of Christ.

I want to give you one extract from one of his recent letters:

> My soul was so overcome. I had to ask God to somewhat lessen the weight of the glory, because the mystical power was so overwhelming. It is impossible for me to describe my joy in the Lord. My cup is overflowing. If I feel in any way depressed I fall at once at the foot of the Cross. Never has the power of the living Christ been so vividly felt as during the last four months; demonstration after demonstration that He was with me at my side.

I dare to put that experience side by side with the experience of the apostle Paul. Both of these men, the apostle and my friend, could sing the surrender song: "The love of Christ throngs me, grips me, carries me on and upward," because each of them could sing the song of praise: "He loved me and gave Himself for me." Paul and my friend became new men in Christ Jesus. Such is the wonder of the grace and love of Christ, and their transformation was only one token of its blessed and transforming work.

But now I turn my question around. What did the love of Christ constrain Paul to do? I will tell you. It moved the apostle Paul to publicly change sides, and stand forth among his fellowmen as a redeemed and confessed disciple of Christ. Friends, that kind of reversal demands a mighty constraint. To stand in the old circle with a new confession, of a new leader, to even confess to a new way of life is not a thing that any man will turn to without great effort. To stand in the old workshop and say, "I love the Lord Jesus Christ," to gather the circle of your own publican friends around and, then, to confess your faith and talk to them about the Lord is no easy thing. To gather the Pharisees around you and tell your old circle of associates that you have given your life to Christ often means that you tread the red way of sacrifice, and it often ends in martyrdom. No man will turn to that road unless he is driven, impelled by a master passionate love

Paul was going to Damascus to arrest the men and women there who loved the great Lover, but on the way to Damascus he himself was gripped and arrested by the same great Lover. When he reached Damascus he found himself among the friends of the great Lover proclaiming Jesus as the Son of God. But that was not all. I always feel—I do not know how far the exegesis is just, but for me it is going to be legitimate—that in one sentence in the early records of Paul's Christian life there is a warrant that gives me a glimpse of a splendid ministry. And the sentence is this: "Then departed Barnabas to Tarsus, for to seek Saul [Paul]" (Acts 11:25). What was he doing there? Tarsus was his old university town. My legitimate exegesis and interpretation is this, that he had gone back to the haunts of his old university that he might stand before the public and confess his mighty change, and tell the men of his old university—if still they sojourned there—that he had become a soldier and follower of the Nazarene.

It is just as if in our own day some young fellow who has not led a very straight or clean life, or at any rate has been indifferent to holy things or even hostile to Christ, should later be captured by the love of Christ. Then he decides go back to Oxford or Cambridge or Edinburgh or Glasgow or Aberdeen or Yale or Harvard in order to tell the young fellows that a radical change had come over his spirit, and that he was going to be an out-and-out disciple of the Lord Jesus. I say that kind of reversal, going back where you are known and telling the people there that you have gotten a new Leader and a new Lover, and that you are beginning a new career with a new allegiance, demands spiritual experience and a moral imperative, and a vital dynamic. They are to be expressed and expounded in the one great central word of my text, "The love of Christ constraineth me."

What else did the love of Christ constrain Paul to do? It constrained him to risk anything and everything that would in any way hamper his loyalty to his Lord. If there was anything that would in the least degree impede the fruitfulness of his allegiance to Jesus Christ, it would have to go. Social prestige, ecclesiastical honors, the hope and prospect of a distinguished career—if need be—all must go! "I have suffered the loss of all things" (Phil. 3:8). Have you weighed that word? "I have suffered the loss of all things." Then this a little later, "And I therein do rejoice, yea, and will rejoice" (1:18). "I do esteem them but refuse, that I may win Christ and be found in Him" (3:8). To a man like that a difficulty is not a menace, a difficulty is not a threat; it is an invitation, an allurement. Every bristling fort is a kind of prospective bread house, and he makes for it as a hungry man would make for a feast.

Is it the dread antagonism of Imperial Rome that looms before him? "I am ready to preach the gospel to you that are at Rome also" (Rom. 1:15). Is it the hostile menace even of death itself? "I am now ready to be offered" (2 Tim. 4:6). He is ready for anything, ready for everything, however crowded the way may be with the ministers and ministrations of the Devil. He is ready for anything, for "the love of Christ constraineth me."

And there again I am not going to allow that page to be a page that has now become obsolete. That same wonderful love is still laying its glorious constraint upon the souls of God's children. It is still arresting them, still gripping them, still thronging them, still carrying them everywhere into the ways of service and chivalry and sacrifice. If only all the tracks of heroism that are now being traced in this very land of ours could just be unveiled, what a wonderful revelation it would be! But when you have heroism of this kind, which is constrained by the love of Christ very frequently, it burns away underground, and you have to do a great deal of wooing to get it to show itself.

Only the other day in a little corner of a paper, printed in the very smallest type on a page that was distinguished by great doings in the field of war among distinguished names of those who had done great deeds and were being rewarded, I read these words: "In far-away Laos, six brick cottages, accommodating 100 lepers, have been dedicated as the first leper asylum in the kingdom of Siam."

Who is going to that leper asylum to minister there? A little handful of women. But have you ever seen a leper? I saw half a dozen of them in one of the lanes of Shechem, very near to Jacob's well, just about fifteen months ago. The human image in their countenance had been almost entirely eaten away. Each invisible spirit was living in a partial corpse. Anything more pathetic and anything more physically repulsive my eyes have never seen. And who is going to minister to these? A little company of missionary women! One of my missionary friends in India, writing me the other day, tells me she is praying and longing that the Lord will send her to Almora that she may work among the lepers. But why do these delicate, refined, and cultured women undertake work like this? There is only one answer. The love of Christ constrains them. Thus, that little small-type paragraph in the corner of my newspaper had a distinction and a glory about it that amid all the glories of our time was not in the least degree eclipsed.

I will lift another veil just for a moment that I may give you one other glimpse of heroic chivalry. It is in Tiberias on the shores of the Lake of Galilee. I think Tiberias is a most appalling place. Sir Frederick Treves, the eminent surgeon, in his latest book, *The Land of Desolation,* has dismissed the little town of Tiberias in about fifty lines. I would like to read you a few of those lines:

> The present town is made up of narrow paved streets, which are more or less liberally covered with filth, for Tiberias is famous for its dirt. The homes are uninteresting where they are not actually ugly. The bazaar is mean and squalid. In short, it is a wretched place. The humbler citizens are the most miserable objects to be met with outside a hospital ward.

Yet in that repellent place called Tiberias, and thus described by one doctor, there is another doctor whom I met, a Scotchman who has been laboring there in Christian chivalry for over twenty years. He is away from all his kindred, from all the privileges of intellectual fellowship, and he moves in and out among the wretched people as a gracious and kindly physician of the Lord Christ. What makes him do it? What makes him do it day after day, month after month, year after year? I can see him now just as our boat was leaving Tiberias to cross the lake as we went on our way toward Damascus standing on the beach waving his hand before turning back again to this dirty, stenchful place to bleed away for Christ. What makes him do it? The love of Christ constrains him.

And now I feel it a great responsibility to speak the closing word of this conference. And instead of being a word of counsel, it shall be a word of challenge. After all these rich and gracious influences, what is the love of Christ going to be upon you and upon me? What kind of constraint? What will it constrain us to be, to do, to bear, to serve?

I would like the last word of the conference to be an unfinished sentence that everyone shall complete for themselves.

The love of Christ constrains me to . . . what?

What is it going to be? The love of Christ constrains me to . . .? It grips me to . . .? It throngs me to . . .?

> Were the whole realm of nature mine,
>   That were an offering far too small;
> Love so amazing, so divine,
>   Demands my life, my soul, my all.

The love of Christ constrains me to . . .?

The Missionary Call of the Old Testament

John Daniel Jones (1865–1942) served for forty years at the Richmond Hill Congregational Church in Bournemouth, England, where he ministered the Word with a remarkable consistency of quality and effectiveness, as his many volumes of published sermons attest. A leader in his denomination, he gave himself to church extension (he helped to start thirty new churches), assistance to needier congregations, and increased salaries for the clergy. He spoke at D. L. Moody's Northfield Conference in 1919.

This sermon was taken from his book, *Richmond Hill Sermons,* published in 1932 by Hodder and Stoughton.

John Daniel Jones

7

THE MISSIONARY CALL OF THE OLD TESTAMENT

Now the word of the LORD came unto Jonah . . . Arise, go to Nineveh, that great city, and cry against it. . . . But Jonah rose up to flee . . . from the presence of the LORD (Jonah 1:1–3).

Arise, go unto Nineveh . . . and preach unto it the preaching that I bid thee. So Jonah arose, and went unto Nineveh. . . . So the people of Nineveh believed God (Jonah 3:2–5).

I DO NOT THINK I can commence my sermon in a better way than by quoting the sentence that Sir George Adam Smith prefixes as a kind of motto to his commentary on the prophet Jonah. Here it is: "This is the tragedy of the book of Jonah, that a book which is made the means of one of the most sublime revelations of truth in the Old Testament should be known to most only for its connection with a whale." Yes, that is the tragedy. Many a passage, many a book in the Bible, has suffered sorely at the hands of good Christian people. They have been treated as armories of proof-texts without any reference to the main lines of the writers' thought. Books like the book of Daniel and the book of Revelation are persistently abused by a whole school of Christian people. They scan them only to discover in them what they imagine to be "signs of the times" without troubling themselves in the slightest about the meaning of Jewish apocalyptic, and without worrying about the historic situation out of which, and to which, the authors wrote. Judging from the way in which some people handle these books you might imagine that the authors were not writing for their own age at all, but that all the while they had the twentieth century in mind.

But, while many books in the Bible have been mishandled and abused, no book has suffered such outrage as this book of the prophet Jonah. All the attention has been concentrated on the story of the whale, as if that were the central thing in the book. Nine out of ten Christian people know it only for that, and would be hard put to it to give any account of the book except that it contains that story. It might be a sort of Old Testament Jules Verne story—a Jewish anticipation of the Tarzan series. We don't trouble our heads about the accuracy or veracity of these modern books. They are confessedly books of the imagination, and we accept them as such. But this book that contains the whale story is in the Bible, and that makes a world of difference.

People have debated and discussed, they have wrangled and quarreled, as to the interpretation to be put upon the story. Literalists have contended that it is just sober matter of fact and have devoted much ingenuity to the task of proving its possibility. Frank Bullen wrote a whole chapter in one of his whaling narratives to prove that a whale could really swallow a man. Belief in the story became a test of orthodoxy, a test even of genuine Christianity. And in the dust raised about the story, the real meaning and purpose of the book were entirely overlooked. And the result of all this again has been that to the average man the book has become a joke and a jest.

And this is sheer tragedy. For this book of Jonah is one of the noblest in the whole of the Old Testament. Of all Old Testament books it is the one that comes nearest in spirit to the New Testament. In its wide outlook, in its insight into God's heart, the only things in the Old Testament to be put in the same class with this book are the concluding chapters of Isaiah and the eighty-seventh Psalm. For in this book God appears not simply as the God of the Jews, but as the God of the whole world. Here His universal love is suggested. Here we can see religion bursting through the swaddling clothes of Jewish narrowness and exclusiveness, and claiming the world for its province. Here we get the truth asserted that the

Gentiles were susceptible to, and would accept, the word of God. It took the vision of the great sheet and his subsequent experience of the actual descent of the Spirit upon Cornelius and his household to convince Peter that God had granted to the Gentiles also repentance to life.

That great conviction had, however, been born in the heart of the writer of this book at least three centuries before. To him had been given the vision of a whole world sharing in the love and compassion of God and responsive to His call. It would do us all good to read the book over again from this point of view. And if the whale episode troubles you—I don't think it need trouble anyone who is acquainted with Eastern habits of thought and composition—then leave that episode out altogether and read direct from the fifteenth verse of the first chapter to the opening verse of chapter 3, so that the central purpose of the book may be clear.

For the central lesson of the book is not that it is impossible to flee from the presence of the Lord or that disobedience inevitably meets with punishment, though these lessons are contained in it. The purpose of the book, as Sir George Adam Smith says, is to illustrate "God's care for the Gentiles and their susceptibility to His word." In short, Jonah is the great missionary book of the Old Testament, and it is about some of the great and simple truths it emphasizes—true now as then—that I want to speak.

There are three points illustrated in this prophecy upon which I wish to dwell for a few minutes. They are familiar enough to us Christian people, for they are simple and elementary, and yet they stand in need of constant reinforcement. Those three truths are these: (1) God's love and compassion reach out to all men; (2) all men are capable of receiving that love and responding to it; (3) men who themselves enjoy the knowledge of God are often strangely and amazingly unwilling to share it with others.

God's Universal Love

The first truth emphasized in this book is that God's love and compassion *reach out to all men*. That is the great revelation of the book. The Jew had been brought up to believe that he had exclusive rights in God. He had been brought up to believe that he was heaven's prime favorite and that his people were God's peculiar people. The people outside the limits of Judaism—the people of Egypt and Assyria and Babylon, people who had often oppressed the people of Israel—were not only the enemies of the Jews. They were also the enemies of God, and their end was destruction and perdition. The discovery the prophet made under the guidance of God's Spirit was that these heathen nations were the objects of God's love, and that the knowledge of God had been committed to Israel, not as a selfish possession, but that Israel might proclaim this truth to an ignorant and perishing world.

All this is implied in the opening sentences of this prophecy: "Arise, go to Nineveh, that great city, and cry against it; for their wickedness is come up before me" (Jonah 1:2). Nineveh was the center of that brutal kingdom of Assyria that had broken Jewish independence and deported and outraged its people. Its wickedness was great. There was no doubt about that; it had come up before God. But God had pity and compassion on Nineveh. The Ninevites were dear to Him, and He would rather save them from their impending doom. "Go to Nineveh," God said, "that great city, and cry against it." All the yearning compassions of the Lord are in that verse. I sometimes think that Nineveh is taken as the scene of the prophet's ministry just because it is an extreme illustration. Its wickedness was great. If ever a people deserved punishment, the Ninevites did. But God has pity and compassion even for them. The pity that yearns over Nineveh is a pity from which none are excluded. The love that pours itself on Nineveh is a love that extends to the lost and the last and the very least.

That is the first fact we must start with: God's love is a universal love; His redemption is a universal redemption. He sent His Son to die for all, and His mercy and compassion run out to all. This is so easily said and yet so hard to realize. It is one of those great commonplaces of religion that, just because it is a commonplace, is desperately difficult really to get into our consciousness. If something could only "stab our spirits wide awake" to a realization of this truth, the missionary problem would be solved. Let me say it quite simply and boldly: God loves everybody. He gave His Son to die for everybody. He wants to save everybody. The people of India and China, the half-developed savage folk of Africa, the child races of New Guinea and the islands, they are all God's children. They are all in His heart and His compassions run out to them.

This is the *supreme motive* for the great missionary enterprise. There are other subsidiary motives, no doubt. I once heard a man appeal for support for missions on the ground that missionary work was *good for trade*. Trade followed the flag; the flag followed the missionary. There was truth in the argument, but it was a poor, base, and ignoble plea. A great spiritual enterprise cannot in the long run be carried on for materialistic reasons.

The necessity of missionary work has been urged on *humanitarian grounds*. It is a nobler appeal, and it tells with curious force upon a present-day congregation, more sensitive as people are to physical distress than to spiritual need. And, let it be said, there is ample ground for this appeal. The dark places of the earth are full of cruelty, and the coming of Christianity emancipates people from the bondage of superstition and fear, from ignorance and disease and death. Life, for instance, has become another thing for the natives of the New Hebrides since J. G. Paton first went there, and for the natives of Calabar since Mary Slessor settled in their midst. Missionary work appeals to anyone and everyone who wishes to heal the open sores of humankind.

The necessity of missionary work in these days is being urged in the interests of *world peace*. The condition of the world is a call to more intense missionary effort. There are great Eastern nations like China and Japan that are going to count, and count for much, in the future development of the world. Unless these nations are Christianized, the "yellow peril" may become a deadly menace. The walls of Leeds a little time since were placard with these words: "Christ or Chaos." Is there any other alternative? Chaos will be the inevitable issue unless the world gets our Christ. The world situation is a call to a new missionary crusade. These are all motives to missions. But they are not the supreme motive. It is back to the supreme motive we must get if missionary work is ever to become a passion with us. The other motives are prudential, humanitarian, but the real religious motive is this—that God loves these heathen people, these ignorant and sunken people. God loves them. God gave His Son to die for them. He will not be happy until He gets these lost children back to His heart and His home.

"Arise, go to Nineveh, that great city, and preach unto it the preaching that I bid thee." There you get the Father's love for His lost children, and His yearning desire to save His perishing children! And India is our Nineveh, and China is our Nineveh, and Africa is our Nineveh. God bids us, too, go to Nineveh and preach the preaching He has committed to us. He bids us go and proclaim this message: "God so loved the world that He gave His only begotten Son, that whosoever believeth in Him should not perish, but have everlasting life" (John 3:16).

The Father wants His children. He will not be happy in His heaven until He gathers them in! That is the great compelling motive for missionary work. "The love of Christ constraineth me," said the greatest missionary of them all—not the challenge of the world, not the miseries of men (though he was not indifferent to them), but the love of Christ. That is the supreme motive. For I can conceive of no man really loving the Father without at the same time loving His children, and I can conceive of no man really loving Christ without desiring to help Him to gather in those for whom He gave His life.

The Capacity for Repentance

The second great truth this book illustrates and emphasizes is this, that all men are capable of *receiving God's love and responding to it*. "Arise, go to Nineveh, that great city, and cry against it," said God to the prophet. But Jonah did not want to go. Not because he thought his message beyond the comprehension of the Ninevites, not because he thought they would reject it, but because he had an uneasy feeling that on hearing it they might repent. And Jonah, hard and bitter Jew as he was, did not want them to repent. He would have preferred to see them the objects of God's wrath rather than the recipients of His grace. And what he feared came to pass. When, for the second time, the imperious summons came to him, "Arise, go unto Nineveh . . . and preach" (Jonah 3:2), and he went, however unwillingly, and preached to the dim multitudes of the city, "the people of Nineveh believed God" (v. 5) They repented, and God forgave them their sin. Nineveh, wicked Nineveh, repented!

Nineveh responded to God's call! And the great and blessed truth all this symbolizes and teaches is this, that none are to be shut out of the range of the gospel message. There are no unreachables or impossibles. The Word, when preached and wherever preached, meets with its response. As Sir George Adam Smith expresses it, "Under every form and character of human life, beneath all needs and habits, deeper than despair and more native to man than sin itself, lies the power of the heart to turn. It was this, and not Hope, that remained at the bottom of Pandora's box when every other gift had fled. For this is the indispensable secret of Hope. It lies in every heart, waiting for some dream of divine mercy to rouse it; but, when roused, neither ignorance of God, nor pride, nor long obduracy of evil, may withstand it."

"The power of the heart to turn"—that is what this book asserts. The power of every human heart to turn and respond to the appeal of the divine mercy—that is the truth it proclaims. It was a noble and splendid bit of theorizing when the author wrote this book. He was arguing from the nature of God and the nature of man. But it is a fact of experience for us. For men have traveled to every Nineveh beneath the sun since the days of Jonah and have preached the preaching committed to them—the preaching of the grace of God in Christ, the preaching of the redeeming passion of God revealed in the Cross. Everywhere the miracle of Nineveh has been repeated, everywhere men have believed in God, everywhere there has been demonstrated *the capacity of the heart to turn!*

I do not know that Christian folk have ever been reluctant to carry the gospel into any particular land for fear the people should repent. From that harsh and narrow exclusiveness, which found satisfaction in the thought that other people were shut out from the mercies of God, we have been delivered. But I am not at all sure that Christian people have not been slow in sending the gospel to this land and that because they felt the people *could not* repent. Either they said the people were so devoted to their ancestral religions that it seemed hopeless to attempt to change them, or they were so sunk in savagery and sin as to be insensible to any and every high appeal. But the experience of the century and half of the modern missionary enterprise has banished that doubt. Nothing has been more moving and subduing than the response the human heart everywhere makes to the preaching of the gospel. Every Nineveh can repent! They have come from the north and the south and the east and the west and sat down in the kingdom of God. The people who have washed their robes and made them white in the blood of the Lamb are of every nation, tribe, tongue, and condition. Everywhere, under the preaching of the gospel, there has been revealed the *power of the heart to turn!*

"Arise, go to Nineveh, that great city." The call came to the ears of William Carey. Nineveh to him was India, that land with an ancient religion and a hoary civilization. To many it seemed a hopeless enterprise, so terrific was the hold their ancient religion had upon the people, so intimately had it intertwined itself with the fabric of their lives. But Indian hearts responded to the preaching of William Carey and his successors. From the devotees of Hinduism Christ gathered His converts. In that unchanging East there has been demonstrated the heart's power to turn.

"Go to Nineveh, that great city." The cry came into the ears of Robert Morrison, and, as interpreted by him,

Nineveh was China. It seemed a foolish adventure, for China had a civilization older than the Christian. But Chinese hearts in turn responded to the preaching of the gospel. In China, Christ gathered His confessors and martyrs. In China there has been demonstrated the heart's power to turn.

Go to Nineveh, that great city." The call came to Robert Moffat, and, as interpreted by him, Nineveh was Africa—dark, benighted, degraded Africa. It seemed a desperate undertaking to go out and seek to evangelize Africa, not so much because there the missionary would find himself confronted by an old civilization, but because there the people were so sunken and degraded and vile. But Moffat went. He went and preached in Nineveh, and the heart of the African responded. Nineveh repented; in Africa Christ gathered His church.

Do you remember the story of Africaner? It was a story so with which Moffat used to thrill his audiences. It was a great story in the days of my youth. Africaner was a sort of robber chief in South Africa. He was the plague and peril of the white settlers in that land. He was the type of the untamable and brutal savage. Scoffers used to tell Moffat to convert Africaner, and then they would begin to believe in missions! Moffat went and preached his gospel to the robber chief. His coarse and brutal heart was touched. He laid aside his savagery, and before long he was accompanying Moffat to the Cape clothed and in his right mind. Nineveh had repented! Nineveh believed God! In that brutal savage converted into a meek follower of Jesus there was demonstrated the power of the heart—the vilest and most degraded and brutalized heart to turn!

And that is why we omit no class, no tribe, from our missionary enterprise. There are no impossibles and unreachables. "The people of Nineveh believed God!" We undertake the enterprise because the love of Christ sustains us. But we undertake it with this faith to sustain us: That there is something in every soul that cries out for Christ and responds to Him when He calls. There are no people so obdurate and sunken that this faculty is destroyed in them. Nineveh—every Nineveh—can repent and believe. In every human heart there lies the power to turn.

The Reluctant Preacher

The third truth I find in the book is that men who know the truth are often amazingly slow to impart it and to share it. Jonah was a reluctant preacher. When the call first came to him he rose up to flee to Tarshish. He did not want to preach in Nineveh. He did not want to give it the chance of repenting. He would rather see Nineveh—the capital of that brutal state that had so ruthlessly oppressed his people—destroyed than saved. So he tried to put all the leagues of land and sea that he could between himself and the great city in which God bade him preach. The religion Jonah believed in was an exclusive, not a universal one. He rebelled against the very thought of Israel's enemies being treated as sons.

Is this without its parallel in the life and experience of the church today? Are we not reluctant preachers still? Is it not a fact that many among us still turn a deaf ear to God's command, "Arise, go unto Nineveh . . . and preach unto it the preaching that I bid thee?" We neither go ourselves, nor help to send others instead of us. Nineveh, that great city, may perish for all we do to help the saving of it.

Our modern heedlessness does not arise from unwillingness, as did Jonah's—though there are those among us who affect to believe that the Christian religion is a religion for the West and not for the East. Our heedlessness at bottom springs from *indifference*. We have no concern at all for the condition of Nineveh. We are not troubled that vast sections of our world's populations live without any knowledge of Christ. We are interested in the political situation in India. We are concerned about the maintenance of the "open door" for trade in China. We can get quite excited in the discussion of the pros and cons of an alliance with Japan. But the fact that the people of India, China, and Japan are ignorant of God's grace to us and all humankind in Christ has never cost us a night's sleep or given us an hour's concern. And this indifference again springs from a lack of religious experience—a failure to realize what the Christian redemption means for ourselves. We are not filled, as the apostle Paul was, with a sense of adoring wonder and gratitude at the grace of God in saving us. We scarcely know what it is to say in a kind of rapture of adoring awe, "The Son of God, who loved me, and gave himself for me" (Gal. 2:20). A church that has lost its sense of wonder at God's amazing love in Christ is bound to be a cold, lethargic, indifferent church.

And that is our deepest want today—to catch again the wonder of God's redeeming love, to realize afresh what it was God did for us when He gave His Son to die on Calvary's hill. The Christian faith is not a morality, it is a redemption. It is not a philosophy, it is a salvation. It is the man who knows what redemption and salvation mean—who knows himself to be redeemed and saved by the grace of God and who will be eager to spread the gospel. It is a deepened and enriched redemptive experience that is our bitter need. That is the secret of the warmed heart and the loosened tongue. And when the church gets the warmed heart and the loosened tongue there will soon be no rebellious and wicked Nineveh left. Every Nineveh will repent and believe, and Christ shall see of the travail of His soul and be abundantly satisfied.

Review of the Whole Charge

Joseph Parker (1830–1902) was one of England's most popular preachers. Largely self-educated, Parker had pulpit gifts that soon moved him into leadership among the Congregationalists. He was a fearless and imaginative preacher who attracted both common people and the aristocracy, and he was particularly a "man's preacher." His *People's Bible* is a collection of the shorthand reports of the sermons and prayers Parker delivered as he preached through the entire Bible in seven years (1884–1891). He pastored the Poultry Church, London, later called the City Temple, from 1869 until his death.

This sermon was taken from *The People's Bible,* volume 18, published in 1902 by Hazell, Watson, and Viney, London.

8

REVIEW OF THE WHOLE CHARGE

Matthew 10

A GREAT MISSIONARY campaign was proposed, and Jesus Christ Himself proposed it. Now what was His idea of such a novel campaign? This is the largest thing He has yet attempted. We may therefore naturally expect to gather from it some hint of His intellectual quality. How does He address Himself to great undertakings? What was His intellectual energy, His moral tone, His propagandist audacity? How will He grip a great occasion? In studying the temptation we thought we could discover from His answers the quality of His character, as from the Devil's questions we formed a deduction as to the Devil's nature. Now from this great and luminous charge, addressed to twelve men in view of a missionary campaign, it is possible we may be able to gather something further concerning the intellectual and moral purpose of the Son of God. To this study I now invite you.

Jesus Sent the Disciples Out in Pairs

First of all, Jesus Christ sent forth His disciples *two and two*. That was a shrewd and gracious arrangement. He might have covered double the ground if He had sent them out one by one. It was not His purpose in the outset to cover much ground. He was more careful at the beginning about the men and the strength and the utility of their service than about the mere acreage of surface that He was to cover. In due time He will lay His hand upon the whole world, but it is early morning now. The dawn is just beginning to make the eastern sky a little gray, and at the outset He says, "You must go out two and two. The lonely heart is soon discouraged. 'Two are better than one. . . . For if they fall, the one will lift

101

up his fellow, but woe to him that is alone when he falleth' (Eccl. 4:9–10)." That was an ancient proverb. It was within the pen of Solomon to write that wise word. It comes within the range of Jesus Christ's purpose to take up our little common proverbs and to give their religious applications and religious securities.

Not only did Jesus Christ send forth His disciples two and two, but each two made up something like one whole. It was as if he had put together hemispheres, and thus made a complete globe of character and service. Look at the names. He sends out Peter and Andrew. Peter, full of fire, daring, passion, enthusiasm, an impetuous man with a strange faculty of leaping and making beginnings of things without any certainty that he would ever continue them to their completion. Andrew—his very name is a character; his very name is a certificate. If he be other than a man, he will be a living irony, for his name means "man," and he was manly in all his conceptions and movements. He was as one who broke up the way with a strong hammer. They will do well together, these two. Probably they will not fall out by the way.

The next couple is James and John. James is elsewhere called a son of thunder—a great rousing, violent voice that came in shocks and claps and bursts. John was idealistic, contemplative. His eyes often settled into a calm, dreamy wonder, and his whole face looking as if his eyes were fastened on God's great eternity. There will be no occasion of difference between two such men; they are well mated. This also comes forth from the Lord of hosts, who is wonderful in counsel and excellent in working.

The next couple is Simon Zelotes and Judas Iscariot. Simon Zelotes—Simon the zealot, Simon the hot coal, Simon the fervent man—was all fire, clothed with zeal as with a garment. Judas Iscariot was cold, calculating, shrewd, representing the secularistic, administrative, executive side of things. If any man could go with Judas, Simon is the man to accompany him. If Judas can be trusted in any company, it was well to bind him to the fire. If there is purification and disinfection to be had anywhere it is in the red flame—so potent is fire.

"What think ye of Christ?" (Matt. 22:42). He did not allow the men to go out two and two just as they pleased, but two and two as He pleased. He sets the stars in their places. He fixes the bounds of our habitation. There is a balance in His hand, and He goes into the detail of every economy He administers. The very hairs of your head are all numbered, and He who watches the night lamps of the heavens watches the small birds that fall upon the earth. We may repeat, therefore, that in this arrangement there was at once great shrewdness and great grace.

Is it not a fact well attested among ourselves that some men ought never to be thrown into association with one another? Each of the men is good, but they ought never to have come into nominal *union*. They do not understand one another. They are out of sympathy and *rapport*. They cannot comprehend one another's purposes and impulses. They are, perhaps, too much alike to be agreeable the one to the other, or there may be something about their dissimilarity that does not admit of immediate reconciliation. There is a want of adaptation between the two, and yet the character of each may be excellent. Matches are made in heaven in the widest sense. God knows all about the law of harmonies and companionships, and He is the wise man who waits until the colleague is found in heaven. I ask you, therefore, in the beginning of this study, to estimate this arrangement as affording some illustration of the compass of mind that proposed this great missionary campaign.

Jesus Sent the Disciples Out Impoverished but Enriched

The next point, which is illustrative of the character of Christ, is in the fact that He impoverished the disciples materially, and enriched them to infinitude of redundance spiritually. Never was master so severe with servant as to all material possessions and equipments. Christ's charge was a process of stripping in the first instance. No man was to have two coats or two staves. He was to take neither gold, nor silver, nor brass in his purse. Everything that could be taken from a man was stripped from him by the very hand that sent him forth. There was no encouragement on the material side. No bribe, allurement, inducement, or promise was given on the side that was purely secular and worldly. And yet, on the other hand, as to the enrichment of the men, why, all heaven was placed at their disposal spiritually. They were to have inspiration, speech, and comfort at every point. Nothing was withheld from them that could give them solace and ennoblement and quietude and the positive triumph of security.

He was a statesman. He took a view that was bounded only by horizons. His plan was a firmament. Our little plans are broken arcs of His great circle. We are indebted even for the little arcs we draw to the great circle that He described. Remember there was no missionary society when Jesus Christ uttered this charge. There was nothing to go by. There was no hint in any human mind of such a scheme as this. We must therefore divest ourselves of all the conceptions and prejudices that we have gathered throughout nineteen centuries, and set ourselves at the chronological point of Christ's planning and thinking, if we would rightly estimate His method of spreading a Christian gospel.

In the case of Christ, poverty was to become a kind of holiness. To have two coats was to break a vow, to have two staves was to be suspected of disloyalty, to have a look of having anything of your own was to be brought under the suspicion of distrust in God. Outward grandeur would have clashed with spiritual nobleness and aspiration. To make the case clearer upon that side, Jesus Christ not only stripped the disciples of everything in the form of an encumbrance, but he further depressed the materialistic side by telling them that they would have blows, taunts, insults, scourgings, hatred of all men for His name's sake. This was a tremendous depression of the material side, an infinite discouragement to Judas Iscariot. It is the same today.

What do you think of this Man? *We* move by making great promises. We inspire by bribing. We encourage by *enriching,* in a material and physical sense. But Jesus Christ stripped every man of the Twelve of everything that looked like encumbrance, or ornament, or personal security, and sent him forth with nothing but—*God.* His kingdom was not of this world. His masonry was not a building up with stone. His purpose was a great spiritual one. Evidently, from this very inception of His plan, He means the spirituality of His kingdom to be distinctly revealed to every eye. The kingdom of God comes not with observation. The kingdom of God is not a material success. The kingdom of heaven is within.

Jesus Sent the Disciples Out Demanding Great Homage to Himself

Then look, in the third place, at the kind of homage that He claimed. It was preposterous, if not divine. There was no other name for it than the name that describes its ridiculousness, if it was not a divine claim. Father and mother must go; sister and brother must be surrendered; houses and land must be abandoned; the world reduced to one pair of sandals and one stout staff. "He that loveth father or mother more than me is not worthy of me: and he that loveth son or daughter more than me is not worthy of me. And he that taketh not his cross, and followeth after me, is not worthy of me" (Matt. 10:37–38). "If any man come to me, and hate not his father, and mother, and wife, and children, and brethren, and sisters, yea, and his own life also, he cannot be my disciple" (Luke 14:26). He Himself was the one inspiration of the disciples, His name the only name they knew or were called upon to breathe. This was the homage He demanded— no oath in mere words, no vow spoken into the vacant air to be lost in its ample spaces, but direct, positive, complete surrender. I do not ask you to form any opinion of the homage itself at this moment. But I do ask you to form your estimate of a man who, in ordering twelve men to do a work, says that if He is not supreme beyond father, mother, sister, brother, houses, land, any man who professes to do His work does it with hireling fingers, with a mercenary and dishonorable soul.

It was a bold claim, and it was most graphically expressed. This was not the way in which an *impostor* would have moved. He would have sought by guile and promise and bribe, by all the tricks known to imposture, to have endeared these men to the cause he wished to propagate. But the impostor has no cause that he wishes to propagate except the cause of *himself*. Jesus Christ had this great cause to propagate: the kingdom of heaven, as first seen in the cleansing of the leper, the healing of the sick, the blessing of the unblessed, and the sending of a plentiful rain upon lives that were perishing with thirst.

Jesus Sent the Disciples Out
to Openly Preach the Gospel

There was another point in His charge that must reckon in the great argument, and that was the command to avoid all religious mystery and monasticism and jugglery in founding the new kingdom. "What I tell you in darkness [or in secrecy, face to face, in this private interview], that speak ye in light: and what ye hear in the ear, that preach ye upon the housetops" (Matt. 10:27). There are no little corners and monastic enclosures and priestly confessional boxes in this great kingdom of Christ. This is no branch of the black art. This is not a question of attainment in priestly mummery and symbolic representation, and things that can be only penetrated and expounded by the initiated and the learned. This is our conception of the kingdom of heaven—and we believe it to be Christ's own—that the Book revealing it is open to everybody, that the Book can now be read in our mother tongue, and that every man is responsible to God directly for the use that he makes of that Book.

Herein I rejoice to believe that we have the truth of God. You may know about it as much as I do, if you will attend to it with your whole soul and study it with your whole affection. I do not believe in any ministerial *class*. There is no minister that knows more or needs know more than the plainest man in society, except it be by some specialty of intellectual gift, or by some opportunity of closer literal study. But as to all that is essential, substantial, and vital in the gospel, I would as lief you consulted the man who sweeps the floor of the church as consult me in my purely so-called "professional" capacity. I have no profession. If I have not a *vocation* then am I nothing in life. We are *all* ministers. Some are speaking ministers, some giving ministers, some sick-visiting ministers, some quiet and sympathetic ministers, but all the Lord's people are prophets. We are only in the apostolic succession so long as we succeed to the apostolic *spirit* and to the apostolic *doctrine*.

The ministerial class must be put down and discouraged by the true spirit of Christian Protestantism. The ministerial class spirit may become the curse of Christendom. I would have everything done in the light. I would have what is called a "layman" preside at the Lord's Supper as certainly as I would have any minister that ever was garbed in the official clothing of the church. Go directly to your Bible and to every honest man you can meet, and get light from all quarters. Know that the church does not represent some little secret trick, some art of spiritual conjuring, but is an infinite gospel of love, welcome, and hospitality to those that are lost.

He was no mean man who delivered this great charge that we have thus from time to time read and studied. He was a grand Man. There is no paltry idea within the whole compass of His charge. There is no heel that can be wounded in this Achillean address. Every word is sublime, and the whole purpose is beneficent. I ask you to call this Man Savior, Lord, King, Priest, and from this day to say you fall within the inspiration of His charge and will be the soldiers of His cross. The church is nothing today if she be not inspired. I will not listen to any toothless old church that does but mumble a literal creed. The church must lay her claim upon my attention by her inspiration, by her power to touch my heart's disease, my life's sharpest pain, my soul's bitterest accusation. Do not let us go forth with symbols and signs and fine traditions, and grandly outlined and highly elaborated faiths and creeds and professions. But let the world feel that we have an answer to all its charges, a reply to all its inquiries—

> A sovereign balm for every wound,
> A cordial for its fears.

Do not let us secrete ourselves in a corner, huddled together like sheep, afraid of a rolling thunderstorm, but let us be out everywhere inquiring, looking, testing, and offering our gospel. Let us translate it into every language. Let us take it into every society—some speaking it as a high philosophy, others breathing it as a gentle blessing, others loving it as a high promise and tender solace, and all displaying it with a chivalrous and useful consistency. Then shall the church, though nineteen centuries old, be fair as the sun, clear as the moon, and terrible as an army with banners.

NOTES

The Missionary's Charge and Charta

Charles Haddon Spurgeon (1834–1892) is undoubtedly the most famous minister of the nineteenth century. Converted in 1850, he united with the Baptists and soon began to preach in various places. He became pastor of the Baptist church in Waterbeach, England, in 1851, and three years later he was called to the decaying Park Street Church, London. Within a short time the work began to prosper, a new church was built and dedicated in 1861, and Spurgeon became London's most popular preacher. In 1855, he began to publish his sermons weekly; today they make up the fifty-seven volumes of *The Metropolitan Tabernacle Pulpit*. He founded a pastor's college and several orphanages.

This sermon was taken from *The Metropolitan Tabernacle Pulpit,* volume 7. Spurgeon preached it on behalf of the Baptist Missionary Society.

Charles Haddon Spurgeon

9

THE MISSIONARY'S CHARGE AND CHARTA

And Jesus came and spake unto them, saying, All power is given unto me in heaven and in earth. Go ye therefore, and teach all nations, baptizing them in the name of the Father, and of the Son, and of the Holy Ghost (Matthew 28:18–19).

WHILE I WAS MEDITATING in private upon this text I felt myself carried away by its power. I was quite unable calmly to consider its terms or to investigate its argument. The *command* with which the text concludes repeated itself again and again and again in my ears until I found it impossible to study, for my thoughts were running here and there asking a thousand questions, all of them intended to help me in answering for myself the solemn inquiry, "How am *I* to go 'and teach *all* nations, baptizing them in the name of the Father, and of the Son, and of the Holy Ghost'!" The practical lesson seemed to me to overwhelm in my mind the argument of which that lesson is but a conclusion, "Go ye . . . and teach all nations." My ears seemed to hear it as if Christ were then speaking it *to me*. I could realize His presence by my side. I thought I could see Him lift His pierced hand and hear Him speak, as He was accustomed to speak, with authority, blended with meekness, "Go ye . . . and teach all nations, baptizing them in the name of the [all-glorious God]."

Oh I wish that the church could hear the Savior addressing these words to her now, for the words of Christ are living words, not basing power in them yesterday alone, but today also. The injunctions of the Savior are perpetual in their obligation. They were not binding upon apostles merely, but upon *us* also, and upon every Christian does this yoke fall, "Go ye therefore, and teach all

111

nations, baptizing them in the name of the Father, and of the Son, and of the Holy Ghost." We are not exempt today from the service of the first followers of the Lamb. Our marching orders are the same as theirs, and our Captain requires from us obedience as prompt and perfect as from them. Oh that His message may not fall upon deaf ears or be heard by stolid souls!

Friends, the heathen are perishing. Shall we *let* them perish? *His* name is blasphemed. Shall we be quiet and still? The honor of Christ is cast into the dust, and His foes revile His person and resist His throne. Shall we His soldiers suffer this, and not find our hands feeling for the hilt of our sword, the sword of the Spirit, which is the Word of God? Our Lord delays His coming. Shall we begin to sleep or to eat or to be drunken? Shall we not rather gird up the loins of our mind and cry to Him, "Come, Lord Jesus, come quickly"?

The scoffing skeptics of these last days have said that the anticipated conquest of the world for Christ is but a dream, or an ambitious thought, that crossed our leader's mind, but which never is to be accomplished. It is asserted by some that the superstitions of the heathen are too strong to be battered down by our teachings, and that the strongholds of Satan are utterly impregnable against our attacks. Shall it be so? Shall we be content foolishly to sit still? No! Rather let us work out the problem. Let us prove the promise of God to be true. Let us prove the words of Jesus to be words of soberness. Let us show the efficacy of His blood and the invincibility of His Spirit by going in the spirit of faith, teaching all nations and winning them to the obedience of Christ our Lord.

I do not know how to begin to preach this morning, but still it seems to me standing here as if I heard that voice saying, "Go [thou] therefore, and teach all nations." My soul sometimes pants and longs for the liberty to preach Christ where He was never preached before. I long not to build on another man's foundation, but to go to some untrodden land, some waste where the foot of Christ's minister was never seen, that there "the solitary place shall be glad for them; and the desert shall rejoice, and blossom as the rose" (Isa. 35:1). I have made it a solemn question whether I might not testify in China or India the grace of Jesus, and in the sight of God I have answered it. I solemnly feel that my position in England will not permit my leaving the sphere in which I now am, or else tomorrow I would offer myself as a missionary.

Oh, do none of you hear the call this morning! You that are free from so great a work as that which is cast upon me—you that have talents as yet undevoted to any special end, powers of being as yet unconsecrated to any given purpose and unconfined to any one sphere—do you not hear my Master saying, in tones of plaintive sorrow blended with an authority that is not to be denied, "Go ye therefore, and teach all nations, baptizing them in the name of the Father, and of the Son, and of the Holy Ghost"?

Oh that I could preach like Peter the Hermit—a better crusade than he! Oh that there were might in some human lip to move the thousands of our Israel to advance at once, unanimously and irresistibly to the world's conquest, like one tremendous tide rising from the depths of the ocean to sweep over the sands, the barren sands, that are now given up to desolation and death! Oh that once again the voice of thunder could be heard, and the lightning spirit could penetrate each heart, that as one man the entire church might take the marching orders of her Lord and go teach all nations, baptizing them in the name of Israel's God! O Lord, if *we* fail to speak, fail not Yourself to speak. If we know not how to bear Your burden or express Your thoughts, yet speak, Lord, with that all-constraining silent voice that well-trained ears can hear and make Your servants obedient to You now, for Christ's sake!

> Awake, thou Spirit, who of old
> Didst fire the watchman of the Church's youth,
> Who faced the foe, unshrinking, bold,
> Who witness'd day and night the eternal truth,
> Whose voices through the world are ringing still,
> And bringing hosts to know and do thy will!

> Oh that thy fire were kindled soon,
> That swift from land to land its flame might leap!
> Lord, give us but this priceless boon
> Of faithful servants, fit for thee to reap
> The harvest of the soul; look down and view
> How great the harvest, yet the laborers few.
>
> Oh haste to help ere we are lost!
> Send forth evangelists, in spirit strong,
> Arm'd with thy Word, a dauntless host,
> Bold to attack the rule of ancient wrong;
> And let them all the earth for thee reclaim,
> To be thy kingdom, and to know thy name.

This morning we shall first dwell a little while upon the *command*. Then, secondly, we shall enlarge upon the *argument*. There is an argument, as you will perceive, "Go ye *therefore,* and teach all nations."

The Command

We must remark, first, what a singularly loving command it is. Imagine Muhammad on his dying bed saying to his disciples, "All power is given unto me in heaven and in earth." What would be his command? "Go, therefore, with sharp scimitars, and propound faith in the prophet, or death as the dread alternative. Avenge me of the men who threw stones at the prophet. Make their houses a dunghill and cut them in pieces, for vengeance is mine, and God's prophet *must* be avenged of his enemies." But Christ, though far more despised and persecuted of men, and having a real power, which that pretended prophet never had, says to His disciples as He is about to ascend to heaven, "All power is given unto me in heaven and in earth. Go ye therefore, and teach all nations, baptizing them in the name of the Father, and of the Son, and of the Holy Ghost."

It is the voice of love, not of wrath. "Go and teach them the power of My blood to cleanse, the willingness of My arms to embrace, the yearning of My heart to save! Go and *teach* them. Teach them no more to despise Me, no more to think My Father an angry and implacable deity.

Teach them to 'bow [the] knees' (Eph. 3:14) and 'kiss the Son' (Ps. 2:12), and find peace for all their troubles and a balm for all their woes in Me. Go and speak as I have spoken; weep as I have wept; invite as I have invited; exhort, entreat, beseech, and pray as I have done before you. Tell them to come to Me if they be weary and heavy laden, and I will give them rest. Say to them, 'I have no pleasure in the death of him that dieth . . . wherefore turn yourselves, and live ye' (Ezek. 18:32)." What a generous and gracious command is that of the text, "Go ye therefore, and teach all nations, baptizing them in the name of the Father, and of the Son, and of the Holy Ghost."

Note, too, how exceedingly plain is the command, "Go ye . . . *teach* all nations." The Roman Catholic church has misunderstood this. She says, "Go, mystify all nations. Sound in their ears a language once living, but now dead. Take to them the Latin tongue, and let that be sounded with all the harmony of sweet music, and they will be converted. Erect the sumptuous altar, clothe the priest in mystic garments, celebrate mysterious rites, and make the heathen wonder. Dazzle them with splendor and amaze them with mystery." But, "No," says Christ, "no, go . . . and teach."

Why, it is the mother's work with her child; it is the tutor's work with the boy and with the girl—"go . . . and teach." How simple—illustrate, explain, expound, tell, inform, narrate. Take from them the darkness of ignorance and reveal to them the light of revelation. Teach! Be content to sit down and tell them the very plainest and most common things. It is not your eloquence that shall convert them. It is not your gaudy language or your polished periods that shall sway their intellects. Go and teach them. Teach them! Why, my hearer, I say again, this is a word that has to do with the rudiments of knowledge. We do not preach to children, we teach them. We are not so much to preach to nations—that word seems too big and great for the uncivilized and childish people— but go and teach them first the very simplicities of the cross of Christ.

And note how He puts it next. Who are to be taught? "Go ye . . . and teach *all nations.*" The Greek have their philosophers. Teach them as they are but children. They are fools, though they think themselves to be wise. There be polite nations who have a literature of their own, far larger and more extensive than the literature of the Christian, teach them nevertheless. They are to be *taught.* Unless they are willing to take the learner's place and to become as little children, they can in no way enter into the kingdom of heaven. Do not debate and argue with them. Do not put yourself with them upon their level as a combatant concerning certain dogmas. Insist upon it that *I am* has sent you—sent you to teach the most erudite and profoundly learned. When you shall claim it, I am with you always to back your claim, and men shall be willing to sit at your feet to be taught the name of Jesus.

I do not know whether *all* our missionaries have caught the idea of Christ—"Go ye . . . and *teach* all nations." But many of them have, and these have been honored with many conversions. The more fully they have been simple teachers, not philosophers of the Western philosophy, not eager disputants concerning some English dogma, I say the more plainly they have gone forth as teachers sent from God to teach the world, the more successful they have been. "Go ye therefore, and teach."

Some may think, perhaps, there is less difficulty in teaching the learned than in teaching the uncivilized and barbarous. There is the same duty to the one as to the other: "Go . . . and teach." "But they brandish the tomahawk." Teach them, and lie down and sleep in their hut. They shall marvel at your fearlessness and spare your life. "But they feed on the blood of their fellows. They make a bloody feast about the cauldron in which a man's body is the horrible viand." *Teach* them, and they shall empty their war kettle. They shall bury their swords and bow before you and acknowledge King Jesus. "But they are brutalized. They scarcely have a language—a few clicking sounds make up all that they can say." Teach them, and they shall speak the language of Canaan and sing the songs of heaven.

The fact has been proven that there are no nations incapable of being taught, no, that there are no nations incapable afterward of teaching others. The African slave has perished under the lash, rather than dishonor his Master. The Esquimaux has climbed his barren steeps and borne his toil while he has recollected the burden that Jesus bore. The Hindu has patiently submitted to the loss of all things because he loved Christ better than all. Feeble Malagasy women have been prepared to suffer and to die, and have taken joyfully suffering for Christ's sake. There has been heroism in every land for Christ. Men of every color and of every race have died for *Him*. Upon His altar has been found the blood of all kindreds that be upon the face of the earth.

Oh! tell me not that they cannot be taught. Sirs, they can be taught to die for Christ, and this is more than some of you have learned. They can rehearse the very highest lesson of the Christian religion—that self-sacrifice that knows not itself but gives up all for Him. At this day there are Karen missionaries preaching among the Karens with as fervid an eloquence as ever was known by Whitfield. There are Chinese teaching in Borneo, Sumatra, and Australia, with as much earnestness as Morison or Milne first taught in China. There are Hindu evangelists who are not ashamed to have given up the Brahminical thread and to eat with the Pariah and to preach with him the riches of Christ. There have been men found of every class and kind, not only able to be taught, but able to become teachers themselves, and the most mighty teachers, too, of the grace of the Lord Jesus Christ. Well was that command warranted by future facts when Christ said, "Go ye . . . teach all nations."

But the text says, *"baptizing them."* 'They are to be taught and afterward they are to be baptized. I know not why it is that we yield to the superstitions of our fellow Christians, so much as to use the word *baptize* at all. It is not an English word, but a Greek word. It has but one meaning and cannot bear another. Throughout all the classics, without exception, it is not possible to translate it correctly, except with the idea of immersion. Believing this, and knowing this, if the translation is not complete, we will complete it this morning. "Go ye therefore, and teach all nations, *[immersing]* them in the name of the Father, and of the Son, and of the Holy Ghost."

Now, I think that our Missionary Society, while it may take precedence in matters of time—for it was the first that was ever commenced with the exception of the Moravians—ought also to take precedence in matters of purity because we *can* carry out this text in every country, teaching first and baptizing afterward. We do not understand the philosophy of baptizing and afterward teaching. We hold that we must teach first, and then, when men are discipled, we are to baptize them. We do not baptize the nations; the Greek does not bear that interpretation. But those who have been discipled we are to baptize into the Sacred Name.

We think that our fellow Christians do serious damage to the gospel by baptizing children. We do not think their error a little one. We know it does not touch a vital point. But we do believe that infant baptism is the prop and pillar of popery, and it being removed, popery and Puseyism become at once impossible. You have taken away all idea of a national godliness and a national religion when you have cut away all liberty to administer Christian ordinances to unconverted persons. We cannot see any evil that would follow if our fellow Christians would renounce their mistake. But we can see abundant mischief that their mistake has caused, and in all kindness, but with all fidelity, we again enter our solemn protest against their giving baptism to any but disciples, to any but those who are the followers of the Lamb.

Throw down her hedges? Give her supper and her baptism to those that are not Christ's people? Break down her walls? Remove her barricades? God forbid! Except a man be renewed in heart, we dare not allow him to participate in the ordinances that belong to Christ's church. Oh! it is a disastrous thing to call unconverted children Christians, or to do anything that may weaken their apprehension of the great fact that until they be converted they have no part or lot in this matter.

Beloved, if you differ from me on this point, bear with me for my conscience will not let me conceal this solemn truth. To you who agree with me, I say, while our other friends can do in some things more than we can—and we rejoice in their efforts and would heartily bless God that they have shown more activity than ourselves—yet we ought to be ashamed of ourselves if we are a whit behind. We are a body of Christians who can fairly and purely teach and baptize. We can obey this command of Christ abroad, as well as at home, without running counter to our practice in one place by our practice in the other. We ought to be first and foremost, and if we be not, shame shall cover us for our unfaithfulness. Again, I say, I hear that voice ringing in the Baptist's ear, above that of any other man, "Go ye therefore, and teach all nations, baptizing them in the name of the Father, and of the Son, and of the Holy Ghost."

I have endeavored to be brief, but I find I have been long, and therefore pass at once to the argument with which the text commences.

The Argument

The argument is this: "All power is given unto me in heaven and in earth. Go ye therefore, and teach all nations."

There are three things here. Christ had suffered, bled, and died. Now He had risen from the dead. As the effect of His finished work, He had as mediator received all power in heaven and in earth. There is no allusion here to His inherent power that is not *given* to him, that is his native right. He has, as God, all power in heaven and in earth. The text relates to Him as mediator. As mediator He did not have this power once. He was weak, despised, and forsaken even of His God. But now, having finished the work that was given to Him to do, His Father honors Him. He is about to lift Him to His right hand, and gives Him, as the result of resurrection, all power in heaven and in earth.

Three things, then, do I find here. First, this is the picture of the church's history, and *therefore* she should teach all nations. Secondly, this is the church's right.

Thirdly, it is the church's might. For all these reasons she ought to teach all nations.

First, this is the church's *picture*. Christ suffers, bleeds, dies. Do you give up His cause? Do you look upon it as forlorn and desolate? He is nailed to the tree. The world abhors Him, fools gaze, and sinners laugh. Do you lay down your weapons and say it is idle to defend such a man as this? It is all over now, He bows His head upon the cross. "It is finished," He says. Do your unbelieving hearts say, "Aye, indeed, it is finished. His career is over. His hopes are blighted and His prospects withered?" Ah, little do you know that His shame was the mother of His future glory, that the stooping was the rising, and that the crown of thorns was in fact the fruitful root out of which sprang the eternal crown of glory. He is put into the grave. Do you say that there is the grave of all your faith could believe or your hope could suggest? He rises, beloved, and His resurrection takes effect and fruit comes from the fact that He died and was buried.

Do you not see the picture? We have been sending out heralds of the Cross these eighteen hundred years. They have landed upon many a shore to die. Fever has taken off its hundreds. Cruel men have slain their scores. From the first day until now, the record of the mission is written in blood. Somewhere or other there always must be martyrs for Christ. It seems as if the church never could plow a wave without a spray of gore. She is still in Madagascar persecuted, afflicted, tormented. Still are her ministers hunted about like partridges upon the mountains, and her blood is dying the shambles of her slayers.

Do you give up all hope? Shall we, as we look upon the tombs of our missionaries, say that Christ's cause is dead? Friends, as you turn over the long roll and read the names of one after another who sleep in Jesus, shall you say, "Let us close the doors of the mission house. Let us cease our contributions. It is clear the case is hopeless, and the cause can never have success!" No, rather, the church must suffer that she may reign. She must die that she may live. She must be stained with blood that she may be robed in purple. She must go down into the earth, and seem to be buried and forgotten, that the earth may help the woman and that she may be delivered of the man child. Courage! courage! courage! The past is hopeful because to the eye it seems hopeless. The cause is glorious because it has been put to shame. Now, now let us gather the fruits of the bloody sowing. Let us now reap the harvest of the deep plowing of agony and suffering that our ancestors have endured.

I think that no true-hearted Christian will ever give up any enterprise that God has laid upon him because he fears its ultimate success. "Difficult," said Napoleon, "is not a French word." "Doubtful," is not a Christian word. We are *sure* to succeed; the gospel *must* conquer. It is possible for heaven and earth to pass away, but it is not possible for God's Word to fail. Therefore it is utterly impossible that any nation or kindred or tongue should to the end stand out against the attacks of love, against the invasion of the armies of King Jesus.

Thus, then, you see a fair argument can be built upon the text. Inasmuch as Christ is to His people a picture of what they are to be, inasmuch as by His suffering all power was given to Him in heaven and in earth, so after the sufferings of the church, the wounds of her martyrs, and the deaths of her confessors, power shall be given to her in heaven and in earth. She shall reign with Christ over the nations gloriously.

We now take a second view of the argument. This is the church's *right*. All power is given to Christ in heaven and in earth. What then? Why this? Kings and princes, potentates and power, are you aware that your thrones have been given away? Do you know it, you crowned heads, that your crowns have been given—given away from you to one who claims to be King of Kings and Lord of Lords? Do you pass decrees forbidding the gospel to be preached? We laugh at you! You have no power to prevent it, for all power is given to Christ in heaven and in earth. Do you say that the missionary has no right upon your shore? The virgin daughter of Zion shakes her head at you and laughs you to scorn. She has right anywhere and everywhere. She has rights in heaven without limit and rights in earth without bound, for all power is given to her head in heaven and in earth. She therefore has a patent, a claim that is not to be disputed, to take to herself all countries and all kingdoms because the power above is given to Christ.

What is that man doing on yonder shore? He has landed on an island in the South Seas. He is an intruder, banish him at once! Sirs, mind what you do, for surely you fight against God. But the man is sent away. He comes back again, or if not he, another. A severer edict is passed this time, "Let us slay him that the inheritance may still be ours." But another comes, and another, and another. Why do you stand up and take counsel together against the Lord and against His anointed? These men are not intruders, they are ambassadors come to make peace. No, more, they are delegates from heaven come to claim the rightful heritage of King Jesus. You, in putting them away as intruders, have denied the rights of Christ. But to deny is one thing and to disprove another. He has still a right to you, and therefore has the missionary still a right to come whithersoever he will, preaching the unsearchable riches of Christ.

Once or twice in my life I have met with some miserable little ministers who, when I have gone into a village to preach, have questioned my right to preach in the village because I ought to have asked them first or to have consulted them. And can Christian men look on a district as their own dominion, and reckon God's servant as a poacher on their estates or a brigand in their territories? Is there any place on this earth that belongs to any man so that he can shut out God's ministers? We once for all put our foot upon any claim so ridiculous. Wherever there is found a man, there is the minister free to preach. The whole world is our parish. We know of no fetter upon our feet and no gag upon our lips. Though kings should pass laws, the servants of Christ can bear the penalty, but they cannot disobey their Master. Though the Emperor should say the gospel should not be preached by any unauthorized denomination in France, as I have heard he has said of late, we care not for him.

What cares the church for a thousand emperors? Their resolutions are mockery, their laws wastepaper. The church never was yet vassal to the state, or servile slave to principalities and powers, and she neither can nor will be. At all the laws of states she laughs and utterly defies them, if they come in the way of the law of Christ that says, "Preach the gospel to every creature" (Mark 16:15). Friends, I say, the church has a right anywhere and everywhere—a right, not because she is tolerated. The word is insult, not because the law permits. The law permitting or not permitting, tolerated or untolerated, everywhere beneath the arch of God's heaven, God's servants have a right to preach. Oh that they would claim the right, and in every place teach and preach Jesus Christ continually!

But now, lastly, it seems to me that the argument of the text contains the church's *might*. "All power is given unto me in heaven and in earth. Go ye therefore, and teach all nations, baptizing them in the name of the Father, and of the Son, and of the Holy Ghost." You have power to teach, so fear not. Let this be your encouragement. You must succeed; you shall prevail. There never lived another man, save Christ, who could say, "All power is given me on earth." Canute puts his throne by the side of the sea, but the waves wet his person and prove to his flattering courtiers that he is but a man. What power have kings over the lightning or the rushing winds? Can they control the tides or bid the moon stand still? Power is not given to man, even upon earth. Much less could any man say, all power in heaven belonged to him. This is a singular expression, one that only could be used by Christ. If any other should attempt to use it, it were an imposition and a blasphemy. But the Lord Jesus Christ can say today as He said then, "All power is given unto me in heaven and in earth."

Let us think, then, all power is given to Christ in providence. Over common daily events He has supreme authority. You have launched upon the sea on a mission voyage. He rules the waves and wings the winds. Fear not, for tempest is His trembling slave. You have come near the shore, but there are hidden reefs and sunken rocks. Fear not, for all power is given to Him in the lowest deep to guide you safely and to bring you to your desired haven. A band of men meet you upon the shore, brandishing their weapons. You are unarmed and have nothing but the Word. You shall now prove that "for they that be with us are more than they that be with them" (2 Kings 6:16). Go, in this your might. All power is given to Christ—power over the wills of men, as well as over the waves of the sea.

But political occurrences prevent your landing on a certain country. Through treaties, or a lack of treaties, there is no room for the missionary in such-and-such an empire. *Pray,* and the gates shall be opened. *Plead,* and the bars of brass shall be cut in two. Christ has power over politics. He can make wars and create peace with a view to the propagation of His Word. He can change the hearts of princes and preside in the counsels of senates. He can cause nations that have long been shut up to be opened to the truth. And, indeed, what a wonderful proof we have had of late that all power belongs to Christ, for human skill has been yoked to the chariot of the gospel.

How wondrously, my friends, have the inventions of man of late years progressed! How could we have preached the gospel to all nations—how could we have even known that America existed—if it had not been that the Lord put it into the mind of Columbus to discover the New World! And how wearisome our life if with the ordinary slow navigation of the ancient times we had to journey among all nations! But now we are carried across the waves so rapidly that distance is annihilated and time forgotten. Truly God has opened up the world and brought it to our threshold. If He has not made a smaller world, at least He has made it more convenient and nearer to our hands.

And then see how countries that once could not be reached have been opened to us. The Celestial King of China, the rebel prince, invites us to come and preach. He does not merely permit—he invites. He builds places of worship. He is prepared, he says, that his brethren should come and teach him, and teach all his subjects, for they are imperfectly taught in the things of God. And the Imperial Sovereign of China, too, though he does not invite, permits the missionaries to go among his millions. There is perfect liberty for us to preach to four hundred millions of people who before had never seen the light of Calvary. And there is India, too, given up to our dominion. The old company, which always impeded us, rolled up in its shroud and laid in its grave. And there are other lands and other places, which once seemed to be surrounded by impassable mountains, into which we have now a road. Oh, for the will to dash through that road riding upon the white horses of salvation! Oh, for the heart, the spirit, and the soul to avail ourselves of the golden opportunity, and to preach Christ where He has never been preached before! All power, then, we can clearly see, over everything in this world has been given to Christ and has been used for the propagation of His truth.

But, friends, let us recollect that power is given to Christ in heaven as well as on earth. All angels bow before Him, and the cherubim and seraphim are ready to obey His high commands. Power is given to Him over the plenitude of the Holy Spirit. He can pour out the mysterious energy in such abundance that nations can be born in a day. He can clothe His ministers with salvation and make His priests shout aloud for joy. He has power to intercede with God. He shall presently send out men to preach, and presently give the people the mind to hear and give the hearers the will to obey.

We have in the midst of us today our Leader. He is not gone from us. If His flesh and blood be absent, yet in body as well as spirit He still lives, adorned with the dew and beauty of His youth. As for the Muhammadan, *his* leader has long ago rotted in his coffin. But ours lives, and because He lives, His truth and His cause live also. We have with us today a Leader whose power is not diminished, whose influence in the highest heavens has suffered no impairing. He is universal Lord. Oh, let our efforts be worthy of the power that He has promised. Let our zeal be in some respect akin to His zeal, and let our energy prove that the energy divine has not been withdrawn.

I wish that I could preach this morning. But the more earnestly I feel, the more scant are my words with which to express my emotions. I have prayed to God—and it is a prayer I shall repeat until I die—that out of this church there may go many missionaries. I will never be content with a congregation, or with a church, or even with ministers, many of whom have already gone out of our midst. We must have missionaries from this church. God's people everywhere will I trust aid me in training young soldiers for my Master's army. God will send the men, faith will find the means, and we will ourselves send out our own men to proclaim the name of Jesus.

It is a singular thing that there are some young men who get the idea into their minds that they would like to go into foreign lands, but these are frequently the most unfit men, and have not the power and ability. Now, I would that the divine call would come to some gifted men. You who have, perhaps, some wealth of your own, what could be a better object in life than to devote yourself and your substance to the Redeemer's cause? You young men, who have brilliant prospects before you, but who as yet have not the anxieties of a family to maintain, why, would it not be a noble thing to surrender your brilliant prospects that you may become a humble preacher of Christ? The greater the sacrifice, the more honor to yourself and the more acceptable to Him.

I have questioned my own conscience, and I do not think I would be in the path of duty if I would go abroad to preach the Word, leaving this field of labor. But I think many of my friends now laboring at home might, with the greatest advantage, surrender their charges and leave a land where they would scarcely be missed to go where their presence would be as valuable as the presence of a thousand such as they are here. And oh! I long that we may see young men out of the universities and students in our grammar schools—that we may see our physicians, advocates, tradesmen, and educated mechanics—when God has touched their hearts, giving up all they have that

they may teach and preach Christ. We want Vanderkists.
We want Judsons and Brainerds over again. It will never
do to send out to the heathen men who are of no use at
home. We cannot send men of third and tenth class abili-
ties. We must send the highest and best. The bravest men
must lead the van.

O God, anoint Your servants, we beseech You. Put the
fire into their hearts that never can be quenched. Make
it so hot within their hearts that they must die or preach,
that they must lie down with broken hearts or else be
free to preach where Christ was never heard. Beloved, I
envy anyone among you—I say again with truth, I envy
you—if it shall he your lot to go to China, the country so
lately opened to us. I would gladly change places with
you. I would renounce the partial ease of a settlement
in this country, and renounce the responsibilities of so
large a congregation as this with pleasure, if I might have
your honors. I think sometimes that missionaries in the
field—if it be right to compare great things with such
small ones—might say to you as our English king did to
his soldiers at the battle of Agincourt, changing the word
for a moment:

> Ministers in England, now a bed,
> Might think themselves accurs'd they were not here,
> And hold their manhood's cheap, while any speak
> Who fought with us upon this glorious day.

Have we none out of our sixteen hundred members—
have we none out of this congregation of six thousand—
who can say, "Here am I, send me!" Jesus, is there not
one? Must heathens perish? Must the gods of the heathen
hold their thrones? Must Your kingdom fall? Are there
none to own You, none to maintain Your righteous cause?
If there be none, let us weep, each one of us, because such
a calamity has fallen on us. But if there be any who are
willing to give all for Christ, let us who are compelled to
stay at home do our best to help them. Let us see to it
that they lack nothing, for we cannot send them out
without purse or scrip. Let us fill the purse of the men
and women whose hearts God has filled, and take care

of them temporally, leaving it for God to preserve them spiritually.

May the Lord, the divine Master, add His blessing to the feeble words that I have uttered. Let me not conclude until I have said, *I* must teach *you* too, and this is the teaching of God: "Believe on the Lord Jesus Christ, and thou shalt be saved" (Acts 16:31). Trust Him with your soul, and He will save you. For "He that believeth and is baptized shall be saved; but he that believeth not shall be damned" (Mark 16:16).

NOTES

The Missionary Debt

Adoniram Judson Gordon (1836–1895) pastored the
Clarendon Street Baptist Church in Boston from 1869
to 1895, and boldly preached the orthodox faith while
many pulpiteers were yielding to the "new truths" of
evolution and "higher criticism." He was a vigorous
promoter of missions and prophetic teaching, and his
ministry led to the founding of Gordon College and
Gordon-Conwell Seminary. "How Christ Came to
Church" was born out of a dream Dr. Gordon had that
made a deep impression on him. He was careful to point
out that the dream was not a "new revelation" but only
contained a special lesson he needed to learn from God.

This version was taken from *The Great Pulpit Masters:
A. J. Gordon,* published in 1951 by Fleming H. Revell.

Adoniram Judson Gordon

10

THE MISSIONARY DEBT

I am debtor both to the Greeks, and to the Barbarians;
both to the wise, and to the unwise (Romans 1:14).

A REMARKABLE SAYING THIS, and not least because those to
whom the apostle declared himself indebted had never
brought any claim against him. Merchants press their
debtors for payment. But debtors pressing their creditors
to allow them to pay an unrecognized claim—what an
extraordinary thing is this in man's dealing with man!
Yet this is what the apostle was constantly doing in his
ministry. To his listeners in cultured Athens, inquiring
why he had come there, and to the rude inhabitants of
Melita, wondering at his message and at his visit to this
island, his answer would be the same: "I have come to
settle a pressing obligation to you, for 'I am debtor both
to the Greeks, and to the Barbarians; both to the wise,
and to the unwise.' Not only my own kinsmen according
to the flesh, but aliens and strangers are my spiritual
creditors. To these I must pay what I owe."

What is the Great Commission but a transfer of obligation from the ascending Lord to the world that He has
redeemed? You would like to express to Him how much
you feel you owe Him for the gift of eternal life; you would
gladly make a royal offering such as Nicodemus brought
to honor His burial. But He is gone and can no longer
accept such personal tokens of affection. Yet provision
has been made that His heirs shall receive what is ow-
ing to Him. And His heirs are all persons for whom He
has shed His precious blood.

Have you never found yourself indebted to one whom
you have never seen and with whom you have had no
direct dealings? A summons comes to you from a perfect
stranger to settle a specified obligation, and you ask in

astonishment, "Who are you that you should make such a demand upon me?" The answer is that "Mr. Blank holds your note for the sum named. He is dead, and I am his rightful heir." That makes all plain. And China's millions, the myriads of India, the dying souls of Africa, and the islands of the sea are importuning us to pay our debt to them.

When such demand is strongly pressed from the pulpit even some Christians ask with astonishment how the claim may be defended. We reply, "Christ is dead, and these are His heirs. They have redemption rights that have been created by the shedding of His blood, and they now exact of your estate a settlement. In appealing on their behalf we do not ask charity; we plead for equity. We bid you deal as honestly with the heirs of Jesus Christ as with the heirs of your own brother who has made you his executor." Is it not a shame that so many well-to-do Christians, whose business pride would never suffer them to be behind a day in meeting their financial obligations, are ready to take the poor debtor's oath the moment you mention the claims of the unevangelized world? They, with ample means in their hands, yet beg their pastor to give them their discharge in bankruptcy.

I stand here in behalf of these heirs of Jesus Christ. As their advocate I am in court to plead their cause and defend His will. Listen to this: "Who will have all men to be saved, and unto come to the knowledge of the truth" (1 Tim. 2:4). He has made provision for carrying out His will, that He "gave himself a ransom for all, to be testified in due time" (v. 6). Matthew Henry says beautifully that Jesus gave all His personal possessions before He died. He gave His peace to His disciples: "My peace I give unto you" (John 14:27). He gave His clothes to the soldiers: "They parted my garments among them" (Matt 27:35). He gave His mother to His beloved disciple: "Woman, behold thy son" (John 19:26). Yes, and the only command He left was of that which could not be given away until after His death.

The title deed of redemption He made over to the world, for which He gave His life. By "the death of the testator" (Heb. 9:16) that legacy is now due. The Greek and the barbarian, the Brahmin of India, and the savage of Africa, the scholar of Japan, and the ignorant peasant of China—all these have a right to claim from the church and to demand of you and me the gospel of salvation, the knowledge of "the way, the truth, and the life" (John 14:6). The Apostle to the Gentiles acknowledged this claim and, at the cost of unspeakable self-denials and hardships, gave himself to meeting it. Yet we are just as truly and just as greatly debtors as was he, and debtors to precisely the same kinds of people. Repudiate the claim if you will, but I warn any of you who do repudiate it that such a course means eternal insolvency when you are called to answer at the judgment seat of Christ.

Deeds do not find their equivalent in mere words. Our obligation was contracted by the sacrifice of Christ; its discharge must be by the sacrifice of self. It is a significant note in the song of the heavenly choir: "Worthy is the Lamb that was slain to receive power, and *riches*, and wisdom, and strength, and honour, and glory, and blessing" (Rev. 5:12). "Riches," mark you, before "honor and glory and blessing." If you were to borrow a thousand dollars from the bank and were to go to the officials when the note became due, and say, "I have called to express my thanks for the loan of that money," I venture to think they would reply, "Pay what you owe us first, please, and then thank us afterward." Let us understand before it is too late that celestial praises are no equivalent for the sacrifice of the Cross. Christ enjoins us to answer His cross borne on Calvary with our cross borne in daily self-denial, His surrender of heavenly riches with our surrender of earthly riches. Like calls for like in the divine reckoning. You cannot balance your books by making music a voucher for money and singing, "Worthy is the Lamb that was slain to receive . . . riches," while you keep your riches to yourselves.

Note the practical turn of the apostle's word in Hebrews. "By him therefore let us offer the sacrifice of praise to God continually, that is, the fruit of our lips giving thanks in his name" (Heb. 13:15). But lest we should conclude that lip service is enough, he adds: "But to do good and to communicate forget not: for with such sacrifices God is well pleased" (v. 16). The praise of giving, the worship of surrendered wealth—this is what God calls for imperatively. Yet how constantly we labor to cheat God out of His dues and to cheat ourselves out of our reward in our manner of bestowing. We say to a brother, "You could give a hundred dollars to this cause and not feel it." That means: "You can shave closely to the edge of self-sacrifice, and yet not touch it. You can bestow charity and yet keep clear of the cross. What ingenuity of self-defrauding! God would have us give so that we shall feel it. More than the money rendered to Him is the mortification of our avarice in giving it. It is not what a contribution nets Him but what it costs us that determines its real value. I know not but that the widow's mite, the giving of which causes her to go hungry a day, is of more value than contributions from the wealthy man's millions, which necessitated no curtailment of his luxuries to bestow.

So I do not urge on you merely this question, "How much owest thou unto my Lord?" (Luke 16:5), but I urge you to pay the debt in kind. It is written of our blessed Lord that "though he was rich, yet for your sakes he became poor, that ye through his poverty might be rich" (2 Cor. 8:9). To make any adequate return we must impoverish ourselves in our luxuries. We must straiten ourselves in our living. We must let our charity go so deep that it hurts. I am eager that we shall all learn what we may of the "sacrifice of giving" while we still have the opportunity. Fasting is enjoined in the Word of God. Why? Does it profit God when we fast? No, but it costs us something. And the things that cost us will be the things that bless us. Whatever humbles this proud flesh of ours tends to lift us Godward. Whatever taxes our self-indulgence tends to enrich our faith. As between the flesh and the spirit, the great objective is to tip the scale toward the spirit. In order to do this we must not only put into the spirit side of the balance spiritual things, but we must take out of the flesh side of the balance fleshly things. A pound of avarice taken out of one side does as much to turn the scale Godward as a pound of benevolence put into the other side. So he who gives until he feels it secures a double blessing—the blessing of gain to God's treasury and the blessing of loss to his own covetousness.

In the Sermon on the Mount we have the so-called Beatitudes of Jesus, but from the Mount of Glory He gives us a "more-than" beatitude. "It is *more* blessed to give than to receive" (Acts 20:35). Christ had claimed this beatitude for Himself. "[He] gave Himself for our sins" (Gal. 1:4). And now He invites us to share this highest beatitude with Him by giving ourselves to Him. Let us give therefore—give ourselves, give our money, give our time, give our all. The sacrifice of Calvary has put an assessment of love on every redeemed soul. That assessment cannot be paid with crumbs shaken from the tablecloth after we have enjoyed a sumptuous meal. It cannot be paid with pennies drawn from the bank in which the pounds are untouched. It cannot be paid from the interest that forever leaves the principal intact for our own use. Redeemed as we have been by the precious blood of Christ, let us treat the Son of God as our creditor to whom we owe a debt, not as a pauper to whom we may dole out alms.

Remember this, too, that God's claims, as well as man's, become outlawed if not settled on time. We hear talk about a second probation for sinners who, while living, neglected their opportunity of grace. I do not believe in that doctrine. Neither do I believe in any second probation of Christians who failed to do their duty to the world in their day and generation. There will be no chance for us to preach the gospel to the heathen after we have passed through the narrow portals of the grave. There will be no chance to give to the cause of missions when our hands are stiffened in death. Skeleton fingers cannot turn a safe key or sign a check or open a pocketbook. The present is our opportunity. Opportunity is but another word for importunity, as though God did beseech you by us to use the present moment for doing all possible for making known the grace of God to all those who have not heard it.

This incident occurred in a bank recently. A plain man, evidently not accustomed to the ways of business, called for the cashier of the bank. "Bank closed at two o'clock," was the gruff reply. "But I called to pay that note of mine." "Too late," was the reply, "it has gone to protest." "But here is the money," insisted the farmer. "Sorry, but we cannot receive it." "What," exclaimed the astonished debtor, "don't you receive money that is due you when I have it in hand?" "No, sir," was the inexorable verdict, "it is too late." And the iron gate was shut in the man's face.

It is a sort of parable and prophecy of what may occur on a larger scale by-and-by. Belated servants will crowd around the judgment seat to pay the dues of which an awakened conscience has now at length reminded them. I see them reaching out eager palms toward the judge. "Lord, I am ready to pay my debt to the unevangelized world, though I have neglected to pay it for so long." "Lord, I desire to give myself for the salvation of the lost, though I am very slow in reaching the decision." And the Savior stretches out His nailed-pierced hand and answers, "Too late! Too late! This is judgment day and not payday. Oh that 'thou hadst known, even thou, at least in this thy day, the things which belong unto thy peace!' (Luke 19:42)."

Every man's duty is chiefly to his own generation. This is why I object to Christians waiting to bestow their money through their wills. They defraud their real creditors in the interest of those to whom they are not immediately indebted. I can imagine some well-to-do Christian coming up to judgment and hearing the Lord's word, "Inasmuch as ye did it not" (Matt. 25:45), and answering with a look of exceeding surprise, "Lord, but I did. I gave five thousand dollars at one time for the promotion of missions." "Examine the book of remembrance," says the judge to the recording angel. And the latter, after searching, replies: "I find nothing to this man's account. When did he give as he claims?" "I put it in my will," the Christian explains. "Alas!" declares the judge. "In that case it is not set down here to your credit. Have you never read that it is according to deeds done in the body that men receive their reward? What is done outside the body does not count."

We learn from Scripture that God works in His servants "both to will and to do of his good pleasure" (Phil. 2:13). To will without doing is not obedience, it is only intention. To do without willing is not obedience, it is compulsion. God has constituted these two as parts of one great obligation, and "what . . . God hath joined together, let not man put asunder" (Matt. 19:6; Mark 10:9). To will what others shall do with your estate after you are dead—others who may have no sympathy with your desires—this is not obeying the command of God. No, how does it read, "Will with thy might what thy will findeth to will"? Rather, "Whatsoever thy hand findeth to do, do it with thy might; for there is no work, nor device, nor knowledge, nor wisdom, in the grave, whither thou goest" (Exod. 9:10).

Again I remind you that just as certainly as "the field is the world" (Matt. 13:38), so certainly the seed time is now. When the apostle writes, "As we have therefore opportunity, let us do good unto all men" (Gal. 6:10), he uses a word that signifies season. The spring time is the season for sowing. Therefore it is our opportunity. The autumn is the season for reaping. Therefore it is our opportunity. So time is the seed plot of eternity. Do with all diligence and dispatch what you ought to do, and do it now. Shall I say, "[For] the night cometh" (John 9:4)? No. The day comes. "The night is far spent," as the apostle says, "the day is at hand" (Rom. 13:12). The Sabbath of the ages is about to dawn. The millennial rest is close upon us. "Six days shalt thou labour, and do all thy work: but the seventh day is the sabbath of the LORD thy God: in it thou shalt not do any work" (Exod. 20:9–10). "There remaineth therefore a sabbath rest for the people of God" (Heb. 4:9 ASV). "Let us labour therefore to enter into that rest" (v. 11).

There are aged men here who have lived through the larger part of this century, and have seen the beginnings and growth of the mighty missions movement. I ask for your five thousands, your one thousands, your hundreds.

You can give them. This is your century. The next will not be yours, and you have little hope of living into it. I importune you not to lose your chance of doing what you may do now. It is for you I am solicitous, more than for your gifts. We need your offering, but a hundred times more you need to offer it, for your soul's sake and for the clearing of your conscience against the day of reckoning. Widows are here with ample property and none depending on them for support. Young men and women are here who are earning ample wages. I enjoin you all to seize this opportunity, which may never come again. And may God help you meet to the full your debt to Him.

NOTES

The Man of Macedonia

Phillips Brooks (1835–1893) was ordained into the Protestant Episcopal Church in 1860 while serving in Philadelphia. He became minister of Trinity Church, Boston, in 1869, and served there for twenty-two years. In 1891 he was ordained Bishop of Massachusetts. He is best known for his *Lectures on Preaching,* which he delivered at Yale in 1877. He published many volumes of sermons and lectures.

This sermon was taken from *The Candle of the Lord* by Phillips Brooks, and published in 1888 by MacMillan and Company, London.

11

THE MAN OF MACEDONIA

And a vision appeared to Paul in the night; there stood a man of Macedonia, and prayed him, saying, Come over into Macedonia, and help us (Acts 16:9).

IT WAS THE MOMENT when a new work was opening before the great apostle—nothing less than the carrying of the gospel into Europe. He had passed through Asia and was sleeping at Troas with the Mediterranean waters sounding in his ears and, visible across them, the islands that were the broken fringes of another continent. We cannot think that this was the first time that it had come into Paul's mind to think of Christianizing Europe. We can well believe that on the past day he had stood and looked westward, and thought of the souls of men as hardly any man since him has known how to think of them, and longed to win for his Master the unknown world that lay beyond the waters. But now, in his sleep, a vision comes and that completes whatever preparation may have been begun before, and in the morning he is ready to start.

And so it is that before every well-done work the vision comes. We dream before we accomplish. We start with the glorified image of what we are to do shining before our eyes, and it is its splendor that encourages and entices us through all the drudgery of the labor that we meet. The captain dreams out his battle sleeping in his tent. The quick and subtle-brained inventor has visions of his new wonder of machinery before the first toothed wheel is fitted to its place. You merchants see the great enterprise that is to make your fortune break out of vacancy and develop all its richness to you, as if it were a very inspiration from above. No, what is all our boyhood that comes before our life, and thinks and pictures to itself what life shall be, that fancies and resolves and is impatient? What is it but just the vision before the work—the dream of Europe coming to many a young life, as it sleeps at Troas on the margin of the sea? The visions before the work—it is their strength that conquers the difficulties, lifts men up out of the failures, and redeems the tawdriness or squalor of the labor that succeeds.

And such preparatory visions, the best of them, take the form and tone of importunate demands. The man hears the world crying out for just this thing that he is going to start to do tomorrow morning. This battle is to save the cause. This new invention is to turn the tide of wealth. This mighty bargain is to make trade another thing. The world must have it. And the long vision of boyhood is in the same strain too. There is something in him, this new boy says, which other men have never had. His new life has its own distinctive difference. He will fill some little unfilled necessary place. He will touch some little untouched spring. The world needs him. It may prove afterward that the vision was not wholly true. It may seem as if, after all, only another duplicate life was added to a million others, which the world might very well have done without. But still the power of the vision is not soon exhausted, the mortifying confession is not made at once, and before it wholly fades away the vision gives a power and momentum to the life that the life never wholly loses.

And, indeed, we well may doubt whether the vision was a false one, even when the man himself, in his colder and less hopeful years, comes to think and say that it was. We well may doubt whether, with the infinite difference of personal life and character that God sends into the world, every true and earnest man has not some work that he alone can do, some place that he alone can fill. We well may doubt whether there is not somewhere a demand that he alone can satisfy, or whether the world does not need him, is not calling to him, "Come . . . and help us," as he used to hear it in the vision that was shown to him upon the seashore.

So much we say of preparatory visions in general. I want to look with you at this vision of Paul's and see how far we can understand its meaning, and how much we can learn from it. A Macedonian comes before the apostle of Christ and asks him for the gospel. The messenger is the representative, not of Macedonia only, but of all Europe. Macedonia is only the nearest country into which the traveler from Asia must cross first. There he stands in his strange dress, with his strange western look, with his strange gestures before the waking or the sleeping Paul, begging in a strange language, which only the Pentecostal power of spiritual appreciative sympathy can understand, "Come over . . . and help us."

But what was this Macedonia and this Europe that he represented? Did it want the gospel. Had it sent him out because it was restless and craving and uneasy, and could not be satisfied until it heard the truth about Jesus Christ, which Paul of Tarsus had to tell? Nothing of that kind whatsoever. Europe was going on perfectly contented in its heathenism. Its millions knew of nothing that was wanting to their happiness. They were full of their business and their pleasures, scheming for little self-advancements, taking care of their families, living in their tastes or their passions. A few questioning with themselves deep problems of perplexed philosophy, a few hanging votive wreaths on the cold altars of marble gods and goddesses, some looking upward and some downward and some inward for their life. But none were looking eastward to where the apostle was sleeping, or farther east, beyond him, to where the new sun of the new religion was making the dark sky bright with promise on that silent night. So far as we can know there was not one man in Macedonia who wanted Paul.

When he went over there the next day, he found what? He found a few bigoted Jews, some crazy soothsayers and witches, multitudes of indifferent heathen, a few openhearted men and women who heard and believed what he had to tell them, but not one who had believed before or wanted to believe. There was not one who met him at the ship and said, "Come, we have waited for you. We sent for you. We want your help." But what then means the man from Macedonia? If he was not the messenger of the Macedonians, who was he? Who sent him? Ah! there is just the key to it. God sent him. Not the Macedonians themselves. They did not want the gospel. God sent him because He saw that they needed the gospel. The mysterious man was an utterance, not of the conscious want, but of the unconscious need of those poor people. A heart and being of them, deeper and more essential than they knew themselves, took shape in some strange method by the power of God, and came and stood before the sleeping minister and said, "Come over . . . and help us."

The "man of Macedonia" was the very heart and essence of Macedonia, the profoundest capacities of truth and goodness and faith and salvation that Macedonia itself knew nothing of, but which were its real self. These were what took form and pleaded for satisfaction. It is not easy to state it. But look at Europe as it has been since, see the new life that has come forth, the profound spirituality, the earnest faith, the thoughtful devotion, the active unselfishness that has been the Europe of succeeding days. Then we may say that this, and more than this, all that is yet to come, was what God saw lying hidden and hampered, and set free to go and beg for help and release, from the disciple who held the key that has unlocked the fetters.

And is not this a very noble and a very true idea. It is the unsatisfied soul, the deep need, all the more needy because the outside life, perfectly satisfied with itself, does not know that it is needy all the time—it is this that God hears pleading. This soul is the true Macedonia. And so this, as the representative Macedonian, the man of Macedonia brings the appeal. How noble and touching is the picture that this gives us of God. The unconscious needs of the world are all appeals and cries to Him. He does not wait to bear the voice of conscious want. The mere vacancy is a begging after fullness. The mere poverty is a supplication for wealth. The mere darkness cries for light.

Think then a moment of God's infinite view of the capacities of His universe, and consider what a great cry must be forever going up into His ears to which His soul longs and endeavors to respond. Wherever any man is capable of being better or wiser or purer than he is, God hears the soul of that man crying out after the purity and wisdom and goodness which is its right, and of which it is being defrauded by the angry passions or the stubborn will. When you shut out any light or truth from your inner self, by the shutters of avarice or indolence that your outer, superficial, worldly self so easily slips up, that inner self—robbed, starved, darkened, not conscious of its want, hidden away there under the hard surface of your worldliness—has yet a voice that God can hear, accusing before Him your own cruelty to yourself. What a strong piteous wail of dissatisfaction must He hear from this world that seems so satisfied with itself.

Wherever a nation is sunk in slavery or barbarism, it cannot be so perfectly contented with its chains but that He hears the soul of it crying out after liberty and civilization. Wherever a man or a body of men is given to bigotry and prejudice, the love of darkness cannot be so complete but that He hears the human heart begging for the light that it was made for. Wherever lust is ruling, He hears the appeal of a hidden, outraged purity somewhere under the foul outside and sends to it His help. Alas for us if God helped us only when we knew we needed Him and went to Him with full self-conscious wants! Alas for us if every need that we know not had not a voice for Him and did not call Him to us!

Did the world want the Savior? Was it not into a blindness so dark that it did not know that it was blind, into a wickedness so wicked that it was not looking for a Savior, that the Savior came? And when we look back can we say that we wanted the Lord who has taken us into His service and made us His children? Tell me, O Christian, was it a conscious want, was it not the cry of a silent need, that brought the Master to your side at first and so drew you to His? "He first loved us!" Our hope is in the ear that God has for simple need, so that mere emptiness cries out to Him for filling, mere poverty for wealth.

I cannot help turning aside a moment here just to bid you think what the world would be if men were like God in this respect. Suppose that we, all of us, heard every kind of need crying to us with an appeal that we could not resist. Out of every suffering and constraint and wrong suppose there came to us, as out of Macedonia there came to Paul, a ghost, a vision, presenting at once to us the fact of need and the possibility of what the needy man might be if the need were satisfied and the chain broken. Suppose such visions came and stood around us crying out, "Help us." You go through some wretched street and not a beggar touches your robe or looks up in your face, but the bare, dreadful presence of poverty cries out of every tumbling shanty and every ragged pretense of dress. You go among the ignorant, and out from under their contented ignorance their hidden power of knowledge utters itself and says "O teach us."

It is not enough for you that the oppressed are satisfied with their oppression. That only makes you the more eager to feed into consciousness and strength that hunger after liberty that they are too degraded to feel. You see a sick man contented with dogged acquiescence and submission, and you want to show him the possibility and to lead him to the realization of a resignation and delight in suffering that he never dreams of now. Mere pain is itself a cry for sympathy; mere darkness an appeal for light.

"Ah," do you say, "that must be a most uncomfortable way of living. The world forever clamoring for help! Those things are not my mission, not my work. If the world does not know its needs I will not tell it. Let it rest content. That is best for it"? But there have been and, thank God, there are, men of a better stuff than you. There are men who cannot know of a need in all the world from the need of a child fallen in the street whose tears are to be wiped away, to the need of a nation lying in sin whose wickedness must be rebuked to its face at the cost of the rebuker's life. There are men who cannot know of a need in all the world without its taking the shape of a personal appeal to them. They must go and do this thing. There are such men who seem to have a sort of magnetic attraction for all wrongs and pains. All grievances and woes fly to them to be righted and consoled. They attract need. They who cannot sleep at Troas but the soul of Macedonia finds them out and comes across and begs them: "Come . . . and help us." We all must be thankful to know that there are such men among us, however little we may feel that we are such men ourselves. No, however little we may want to be such men.

But let us come a little nearer to the truth that we are studying. It seems to me that all that we have said about the man of Macedonia includes the real state of the case with reference to the essential need of the human soul for the gospel. We often hear of the great cry of human nature for the truth of Christ, man craving the Savior. What does it mean? The world moves on and every face looks satisfied. Eating and drinking, working and studying, loving and hating, struggling and enjoying—those things seem to be sufficient for men's wants. There is no discontent that men will tell you of. They are not conscious of a need. I stop you, the most careless hearer in the church tonight, as you go out and say, "Are you satisfied?" And honestly you answer, "Yes! My business and my family, they are enough for me." "Do you feel any need of Christ?" And honestly you answer, "No! Sometimes I fear that it will go ill with me by and by if I do not seek Him, but at present I do not want Him. I do not see how I should be happier if I had Him here." That is about the most honest answer that your heart would make.

But what then? Just as below the actual Macedonia that did not care for Paul nor want him, there was another possible, ideal Macedonia that God saw and called forth and sent in a visionary form to beg the help it could not do without. So to that civil, flippant answerer of my question at the church door I could say: "Below this outer self of yours that is satisfied with family and business, there is another self that you know nothing of but which God sees. This He values as your truest and deepest self, which to His sight is a real person pleading so piteously for help that He has not been able to resist its pleading. So He has sent His ministers, His Bible, even Himself to satisfy it with that spiritual aid which it cannot do without." I can imagine a look of perplexity and wonder, a turning back, an inward search for this inner self, a strange, bewildered doubt whether it exists at all.

And yet, this coming forth of inner selves with their demands, is it not the one method of all progress? What does it mean when a slave, long satisfied with being fed and housed and clothed, some day comes to the knowledge that he was meant to be free and can rest satisfied as a slave no longer? What is it when the savage's inner nature is touched by the ambition of knowledge and he cannot rest until he grows to be a scholar? What is it when a hard, selfish man's crust is broken, and a sensitive, tender soul uncovered, which makes life a wretched thing to him from that moment unless he has somebody besides himself to love and help and cherish? These men would not believe an hour before that such appetites and faculties were in them. But God knew them and heard them all the time. Long before the men dreamed of it themselves, the slave was crying out to Him for freedom, the savage for culture, and the tyrant for love. Now is it strange that, also unknown to you, there should be other appetites and faculties in you which need a satisfaction? The Bible says there are. Experience says there are. Let us see if we can find some of them.

The first need is a God to love and worship. Anybody who looks wisely back into history sees, I think, regarding man's need of a God to love and worship, just what I have stated to be true. Not that man was always seeking God, or always miserable when he did not find Him. One sees multitudes of men, and sometimes whole periods or whole countries, who seem to have no sense of want whatsoever, to have settled down into the purest materialism and the most utter self-content. But he also sees indications everywhere that the need was present, even where the want was not felt. He sees the idea of God keeping a sort of persistent foothold in the human heart, which proves to him that it belongs there. Whether the heart wants it or not, it and the heart are mates made for one another, and so tending toward each other by a certain essential gravitation, whatever accidental causes may have tried to produce an estrangement between them.

Take one such indication only, a very striking one, I think. There is in man a certain power of veneration, of awe, of adoration. This has always showed itself. In all sorts of men, in all sorts of places, it has broken out, and men have tried to adapt it to all sorts of objects, to satisfy it with all sorts of food. The idolater has offered to his faculty of reverence his wooden idol and said, "There, worship that." The philosopher has offered it his abstract truth and said, "Venerate that." The philanthropist has offered it his ideal humanity and said, "Worship that." And one result has always followed. Everywhere where nothing higher than the idol, the theory, or the humanity was offered for the reverence to fasten on, everywhere where it was offered no one supreme causal God, not merely the object of reverence has ceased to be reverenced, but the very power of reverence itself has been dissipated and lost. Idolatry, philosophy, philanthropy alike have grown irreverent, and man has lost and often come to despise that faculty of venerating and submissive awe, the awe of love, for which he found no use. If this be true, that there is a faculty in man that dies out on any other food and thrives only on the personal Deity, then have we not exactly what I tried to describe, a need of which one may be utterly unconscious and, yet, which is no less a need crying, though the man does not hear it, for supply?

This is precisely the ground that I would take with any thoughtful man who told me seriously and without flippancy that he felt no want of God, that he felt no lack in the absence of relations between his life and that of a supreme infinite Father. "Yes," I would say, "but there is in you a power of loving awe that needs infinite perfection and mercy to call it out and satisfy it. There is an affection that you cannot exercise toward any imperfect being. It is that mixture of admiration and reverence and fear and love that we call worship. Now ask yourself, Are you not losing the power of worship? Is it not dying for want of an object? Are you not conscious that a power of the soul, which other men use and which you used once perhaps, is going from you? Are you not substituting critical, carefully limited, philosophical, partial approbations of imperfect men and things for that absolute, unhindered, whole-souled outpouring of worship that nothing but the perfect can demand or justify? If this power is not utterly to die within you, do you not need God? If you are not to lose that highest reach of love and fear where, uniting, they make worship, must you not have God? Lo! before this expiring faculty the personal God comes and stands, and it lifts up its dying hands to reach after Him. It opens its dying eyes to look upon Him, as when a man is perishing of starvation the sight of bread summons him back to life. He need not die, but live, for here is his own life-food come to him."

Woe to the man who loses the faculty of worship, the faculty of honoring and loving and fearing not merely something better than himself, but something that is the absolute best, the perfect good, his God! The life is gone out of his life when this is gone. There is a cloud upon his thought, a palsy on his action, a chill upon his love. Because you must worship, therefore you must have God.

But more than this. Every man needs not merely a God to worship, but also, taking the fact that meets us everywhere of an estrangement by sin between humankind and God, every man needs some power to turn him and bring him back—some reconciliation, some Reconciler, some Savior for his soul. Again, I say, he may not know his need, but nonetheless the need is there. But, if a man has reached the first want and really is desiring God, then I think he generally does know, or in some vague way suspect, this second want and does desire reconciliation. It is so natural!

Two of you, who have been friends, have quarreled. Your very quarrel, it may be, has brought out to each of you how much you need each other. You never knew your friend was so necessary to your comfort and your happiness. You cannot do without him. Then at once, "How shall I get to him?" becomes your question. O the awkwardness and difficulty, the stumbling and shuffling and blundering of such efforts at return. Men are afraid and ashamed to try. They do not know how they will be received. They cannot give up their old pride. Rebellious tempers and bad habits block the way. I doubt not, so frequent are they, that there are people here tonight who are stumbling about in some such bog of unsettled quarrel, longing to get back to some friend whom they value more in their disagreement than even in the old days of unbroken peace. Their whole soul is hungering for reconciliation. The misery of their separation is that each at heart desires what neither has the frankness and the courage to attain.

Now, under all outward rebellion and wickedness, there is in every man who ought to be a friend of God, and that means every man whom God has made, a need of reconciliation. To get back to God, that is the struggle. The soul is Godlike and seeks its own. It wants its Father. There is an orphanage, a homesickness of the heart that has gone up into the ear of God, and called the Savior, the Reconciler, to meet it by His wondrous life and death. I, for my part, love to see in every restlessness of man's moral life everywhere, whatever forms it takes, the struggles of this imprisoned desire. The reason may be rebellious, and vehemently cast aside the whole story of the New Testament, but the soul is never wholly at its rest away from God. Does this not put it most impressively before us? Is it not something at least to startle us and make us think, if we come to know that the very God of heaven saw a want, a struggle, a longing of our souls after Himself, which was too deep, too obscure, too clouded over with other interests for even us to see ourselves, and came to meet that want with the wonderful manifestation of the incarnation, the atonement?

We hear of the marvelous power of the gospel, and we come to doubt it when we see the multitudes of unsaved men. But it is true. The gospel is powerful, omnipotent. A truth like this, thoroughly believed and taken in, must melt the hardest heart and break down the most stubborn will. It does not save men simply because it is not taken in, not believed. The gospel is powerless, just as the medicine that you keep corked in its vial on the shelf is powerless. If you will not take it, what does it matter what marvelous drugs have lent their subtle virtues to it? Believe and you are saved. Understand and know, and thoroughly take home into your affection and your will, the certain truth that Christ saw your need of Him when you did not know it yourself and came to help you at a cost past all calculation—really believe this and you must be a new man and be saved.

I would like to point out another of the needs of man that God has heard appealing to Him and has satisfied completely. I know that I must speak about it very briefly. It is the need of spiritual guidance, and it is a need whose utterance not God's ear alone can hear. Every man hears it in the race at large and hears it in his brethren, however deaf he may be to it in himself. I think there never was a materialist so complete that he did not realize that the great mass of men were not materialists but believed in spiritual forces and longed for spiritual companies. He might think the spiritual tendency the wildest of delusions, but he could not doubt its prevalence. How could he? Here is the whole earth full of it. Language is all shaped upon it. Thought is all saturated with it. In the most imposing and the most vulgar methods, by solemn oracles and rocking tables, men have always been trying to put themselves into communication with the spiritual world, and to get counsel and help from within the physical.

And if we hear the cry from one another, how much more God hears it. Do you think, poor stumbler, that God did not know it when you found no man to tell you what you ought to do in a perplexity which, as it rose around you, seemed, as it was, unlike any bewilderment that had ever puzzled any man before? Do you think, poor sufferer, that God did not hear it when in your sickness and pain men came about you with their kindness, fed you with delicacies, and spread soft cushions under the tortured body, and all the time the mind diseased, feeling so bitterly that these tender cares for the body's comfort did not begin to touch its spiritual pain, lay moaning and wailing out its hopeless woe? Do you think now, my friend, when you have a hard duty to do, a hard temptation to resist—when you have felt all about you for strength, called in prudence and custom and respectability and interest to keep you straight, and found them all fail because by their very nature they have no spiritual strength to give; when now you stand just ready to give way and fall, ready to go tomorrow morning and do the wrong thing that you have struggled against so long— do you think that God does not know it all and does not hear the poor frightened soul's cry for help against the outrage that is threatening her, and has not prepared a way of aid?

The power of the Holy Spirit—an everlasting spiritual presence among men! What but that is the thing we want? That is what the old oracles were dreaming of and what the modern spiritualists tonight are fumbling after. The power of the Holy Spirit by which every man who is in doubt may know what is right, every man whose soul is sick may be made spiritually whole, every weak man may be made a strong man, that is God's one sufficient answer to the endless appeal of man's spiritual life. The Holy Spirit is God's one great response to the unconscious need of spiritual guidance, which He hears crying out of the deep heart of every man.

I hope that I have made clear to you what I mean. I desire that we might understand ourselves and see what we might be—no, see what we are. While you are living a worldly and a wicked life, letting all sacred things go, caring for no duty, serving no God, there is another self, your possibility, the thing that you might be, the thing that God gave you a chance to be. That self, wronged and trampled on by your recklessness, escapes and flies to God with its appeal: "O, come and help me. I am dying. I am dying. Give me Yourself for my Father. Give me Your Son for my Savior. Give me Your Spirit for my guide." So your soul pleads before God. It pleads with a pathos all the more piteous in his ears because you do not hear the plea yourself. It pleads with such sacred prevalence that the great merciful Heart yields and gives all that the dumb appeal has asked.

What does it mean? Here is the gospel in its fullness. Here is God for you to worship. Here is Christ to save you. Here is the Comforter. Have you asked for them, my poor careless friend, that here they stand with such profusion of blessing waiting to help you? "Ah, no," you say, "I never asked." Suppose, when Paul landed in Macedonia, he had turned to the careless group who watched him as he stepped ashore and said, "Here am I. You sent for me. Here am I with the truth, the Christ you need"—what must their answer have been? "O, no, you are mistaken. We never sent for you. We do not know you. We do not want you!" Yet they had sent. Their needs had stood and begged him to come over out of the lips of that mysterious man of Macedonia. And when they came to know this, they must have found all the more precious the preciousness of a gospel that had come to them in answer to a need they did not know themselves.

And so your needs have stood, and they are standing now before God. They have moved Him to deep pity and care for you. And He has sent the supply for them before you knew you wanted it. And here it is: a God to worship, a Savior to believe in, a Comforter to rest upon. O, if you ever do come, as I wish to God that you might come tonight, to take this mercy and let your thirsty soul drink of this water of life, then you will feel most deeply the goodness that provided for you before you even knew that you needed any such provision. Then you will understand those words of Paul: "God commendeth His love toward us, in that, while we were yet sinners, Christ died for us" (Rom. 5:8).

Until that time comes, what can God do but stand and call you and warn you and beg you to know yourself. "Because thou sayest, I am rich, and increased with goods, and have need of nothing; and knowest not that thou art wretched, and miserable, and poor, and blind, and naked: I counsel thee to buy of me gold tried in the fire, that thou mayest be rich. . . . Behold, I stand at the door and knock: If any man hear my voice, and open the door, I will come in to him, and will sup with him, and he with me" (Rev. 3:17–18, 20).

NOTES

NOTES

NOTES

NOTES